GAMES
CHILDREN
SHOULD PLAY

GAMES CHILDREN SHOULD PLAY

SEQUENTIAL LESSONS FOR TEACHING COMMUNICATION SKILLS IN GRADES K–6

Mary K. Cihak

Barbara Jackson Heron

Scott, Foresman and Company
Glenview, Illinois
London

The games children play
—being seldom just that,
But rather their practice
—for grown-up-ness,
This book is dedicated to young ones'
—play/practice
That these and later years may be
—somehow less lonely, less helpless
Since they've learned to play these games.

Contents

3 LEARNING TO LISTEN 42

4 GETTING THE MESSAGE ACROSS WITHOUT WORDS 61

5 GETTING THE MESSAGE ACROSS WITH WORDS 92

6 SOLVING PROBLEMS 126

7 BECOMING ASSERTIVE 160

Preface

Busy, tired, but concerned caring teachers and counselors—we've meant this book for you. It is yours if you believe that students can be *taught* to communicate clearly and to make conscious changes in their behavior. It is yours if you believe, as we do, that learning to listen, speak, and problem solve is surely as basic as learning to read, add, and punctuate a sentence.

This year-long sequential plan for teaching communication skills is intended for you to use with an entire class or with a small group of students in the elementary grades. Lessons are gradated in levels of sophistication, but low readability levels throughout the units encourage the active participation of students whose academic skills may be lower than their interest levels.

Games Children Should Play grew out of a need we perceived in our own students, the need to be taught effective ways of relating to others. This work has roots in the writings of such masters as Rogers, Glasser, Simon, Kohlberg, and Bach. It reflects much that is now in the "oral tradition" of group-dynamics training, and it draws from the ideas of fellow teachers, student teachers, and our students themselves. In drawing ideas from these sources, we have attempted to place in natural sequence and to systematize the teaching of interpersonal skills.

We have written the text as an "in-hand" manual, with our emphasis upon immediate, practical classroom use. Lessons have clearly stated goals, need few materials, and require little additional preparation. For those of you who wish to pursue the rationale and scope of our topics in greater depth, we include a bibliography of texts that discusses the theories upon which our work is based.

We hope you will have the pleasure, as we have had, of seeing students gain skills for growing.

Acknowledgments

The authors wish to acknowledge the contributions made to this book by each of the following people:

Alfred Wright Jackson, our proofreader, who when asked that a chapter be proofread "yesterday," obligingly turned back the clock.

Kay Paumier, who edited copy, and Billy Raymond Heron, who offered the book title and countless helpful suggestions.

Claire Evraets, who typed our first, first draft, and Edna McLaughlin, who rescued the later editions.

Althalee Berg and teachers of Chico Unified School District, whose enthusiasm during our workshops encouraged us onwards.

Members of the staff of California State University at Chico, for support and practical advice.

The Heron family, Bill, Bruce, Janet, and Randall, and mother Gladys Pitt Jackson, who shared Barbara with a typewriter.

Leaders in the field of affective education whose works motivated our own, especially Sidney Simon, Howard Kirschenbaum, Robert and Isabel Hawley, and Leland Howe. We acknowledge their contribution to educational history as well as to our own personal histories.

Student teachers who inspired specific lessons: Madelyn Burke (for "Our Own Jack-o'-Lantern"), Victoria Haro (for "A Christmas Ornament"), Chester Obgorn (for "Let's Tell a Story"), and Robyn McDonald (for "The Picnic").

ABOUT THE AUTHORS

MARY K. CIHAK, M.A., is an educational psychologist employed in the Paradise, California public schools. She has been an elementary and junior high school teacher and counselor, as well as a school administrator. She currently maintains a private consulting and counseling practice.

BARBARA JACKSON HERON, M.A., has worked as an elementary school teacher for 14 years and is currently employed in Chico, California schools. In addition to classroom teaching, she conducts inservice programs designed to help educators teach children communication skills.

Introduction
Growin' Up Ain't All That Easy

Have you sat in the midst of unpaid bills, wishing for those years you had an allowance? Have you studied wrinkles in the mirror, remembering the junior prom? Have you watched the moving van relocate you, yet another time, thinking of the neighborhood gang when you were nine?

Time often leaves adults with carefully selected memories—images of the first home run, the first date, the first "A" in geometry. Perhaps some envy of youth filters memories: the young, to those who are not, may only appear to be free and vital. Yet when grown-ups allow themselves a more honest looking back, mixed with the victories of the past they see also the closed neighborhood circles, the triangles that left them out, the slamming doors, painful conversations with adults, false accusations linked to an inability to explain. Childhood in any generation means clumsiness and helplessness as well as excitement and energy.

Affective education, the feeling or emotional aspects of learning, grew in popularity from just such looking back. Adult awareness and human potential movements have lead many to feel that for all our national progress, we are an emotionally backward people, finding the expression of feelings difficult, sensing that poor communication lies at the base of family and social distress, wishing we'd learned to understand ourselves and others before we became thirty-five—or sixty-five.

Looking back brings questions: what kind of education could have made us more aware, more expressive, more confident, more altruistic? What kind of education could have reduced the helplessness of being four feet tall and jumbled inside with conflicting feelings and loyalties?

Interest in improving children's social and emotional education has risen at the same time that concern for children's mental health has increased. The National Association of Mental Health insists "growin' up ain't all that easy" and cites statistics to prove its point. Ten percent of all school-age children have emotional problems requiring psychiatric help. As many as three times that number of children need lesser forms of counseling intervention. Few educators or parents would disagree with the idea that nearly all children need assistance in developing interpersonal skills. Whether a child needs to learn to maintain eye contact during conversation or to choose a solution from among several alternatives, that need if unmet may stand in the way of academic, social, or career growth.

FRILL OR ESSENTIAL?

Today's child has perhaps even more decisions to make in his or her lifetime, more strangers to meet in this mobile world, more loneliness to combat, than we adults have encountered. Interpersonal skills are demanded to a new extent at home, at school, in the neighborhood, and will be later on the job and in future families. Teaching communication skills can no longer be viewed as merely an interesting innovation, a frill to be banished during a "return to basics." Indeed, skills of listening and speaking are basic to academic success itself.

Most important, personal and societal tragedies may stem from children's lack of interpersonal skills. Juvenile delinquency, drug and alcohol abuse, and early pregnancies are most likely all related to the young person's inability to cope with society, school, or home.

The coping skills needed include: becoming aware of one's own feelings, expressing feelings and needs, reading nonverbal cues to determine others' feelings, predicting consequences of behavior, and resolving disputes verbally. The young person faced with pressure to use drugs or join gangs needs the ability to make decisions as well as to assertively say "no."

Delinquent behavior, particularly youthful violence, is considered "acting out" by psychologists. To teach young people how to express *in words* what they feel and desire helps them to "speak out" rather than "act out" conflicts at school and home. To teach students how to find alternative solutions to a problem helps them to recognize that they have options in their lives.

The crises affecting young people today are not confined to older teenagers. It is not enough for school districts to offer communications training in high schools alone. There is a steady increase in the use of drugs by the very young, including elementary-aged students. Children between the ages of eight and ten may in fact be highly susceptible because of their strong need to conform with a peer group. Childhood prostitution and pornography rely for their victims upon young people who lack independence. Teaching very young children to be able to make and express healthy decisions is essential.

WHAT IS AFFECTIVE EDUCATION?

We define affective education as education that focuses on nurturing the emotional life of the child.

One whole level of affective education takes place without any formal program. That level, the informal level, includes the elements of "atmosphere," the often intangible feeling-tone of a school. It encompasses nearly everything, for the emotional life of the child can be nurtured or tarnished by such factors as report cards, instructional styles, methods of discipline, bulletin boards, sports programs, and the extent of mainstreaming.

Most important, affective education occurs informally when the student observes the adults at school. The child watches the facial expressions of the school secretary and hears the tone of voice of the custodian. The child learns communication skills from the ways teachers talk to him or her, to other teachers, or to the principal. The child learns problem-solving skills through the methods adults use to solve problems; he or she learns to celebrate when a teacher's laughter is mixed with affection. For the child, then, affective education occurs on one level when the child observes the relationships among surrounding adults. The child absorbs the "feel" of the school, learning about nonverbal and verbal communication styles long before any formal instruction.

These environmental factors are vitally important. But they do not stand alone. A pleasant environment does not independently spawn children who communicate well. Teachers would never merely hope that students could learn to use consonant blends because they have a colorful bulletin board about them. Curriculum guides, pretests, posttests, competency assessments—educators ordinarily leave little to chance. Behavioral objectives specify expectations ranging from the mastery of addition combinations to the running of the sixty-yard dash. Educators formally teach reading, math, spelling skills, yet those same teachers may spend hours pleading with students to speak with each other respectfully, begging them to listen, hoping that their little self-concepts will flourish. The chance factor in classrooms is surely the highest in the area of affective education. There is probably no other area of curriculum in which we teach so little and yet demand so much:

> "He interrupts every time I talk to someone else."
> "She never looks me in the eye when I talk to her."
> "He is constantly tattling or blaming someone else."

Rarely do we systematically, patiently, determinedly teach behavior. Children are expected to listen, to behave well in groups, to solve problems without "slugging." They don't always. Children who can't decode vowel sounds or do long division are taught vowel sounds and long division. Children who can't catch a ball or draw a circle are taught to catch a ball and draw a circle. There is a precision and sequence present in other teaching that is lacking in the instruction of social learning. To teach vowel sounds, instructors don't begin with cursive letter formation. Yet to teach listening skills they may start with lectures on respect and shortly thereafter end with threats of punishment.

Several commercial programs and publications provide direction to affective education. For example, Glasser's classroom meetings, Palomares and Balls' Human Development Program, Simon's Values Clarification program, and Science Research Associates' Focus series lend structure to a teacher's efforts to improve children's social skills. Direct, formal instruction in interpersonal communication skills supplements the informal teaching that the total school environment provides.

FORMAL TEACHING OF INTERPERSONAL SKILLS

The lessons in *Games Children Should Play* are structured upon "Steps in Effective Planning" outlined by Madeline Hunter and Doug Russell of the University of California at Los Angeles Laboratory School. Lest teaching be unfocused and learning incidental, Hunter and Russell stress the science of teaching, insisting that science frees the teacher to be creative and intuitive in instruction.

Preliminary to planning a lesson in any subject area, the teacher diagnoses both general class (or group) needs and the way in which individual children's needs deviate from group needs. Teaching communication skills is no exception. In *Games Children Should Play*, sections at the beginning of each chapter cue a teacher as to which level to employ with certain children. Considerations of students' ages, maturity, moral-development level, and reading skills all aid in determining appropriate beginning lessons. Observation of students' progress throughout the course determines which lessons need to be reviewed or recycled. Performance of skills within the affective education class period itself cannot be the sole criterion for students' having learned specific skills. Rather, do the postures of listening transfer to sharing time? Do children use "I" messages when expressing their feelings over playground disputes? Diagnosis, then, leads to the ordered steps of the lesson.

STEPS IN EFFECTIVE LESSON PLANNING

Beginning with readiness for the lesson and concluding with reinforcement throughout the day, the following steps guide formal instruction in the lessons of this text:

1. *Anticipatory set.* Creating a mental set or readiness for the lesson precedes instruction and can take many forms. Sometimes, readiness may require a review of previous or related lessons. Other days, an opening discussion may focus on problems, such as playground conflicts or disputes within the classroom for which the particular lesson may offer solutions. Readiness may be achieved by warm-up drills, as when nonverbal charades are used to build the concentration demanded for higher-level role plays. Journal writing can precede formal instruction, setting a quiet stage for the lesson. In choosing a readiness activity, teachers need to pay careful attention to the mood and type of anticipation they intend to create.

2. *Stated objective.* Stating the objective of the lesson to children helps them focus on the purpose of the activity. In teaching interpersonal skills, it is fairly simple to link the goal of the lesson with its significance in later life. One may explain to students, for example, "By the end of this lesson, you will be able to keep eye contact with a speaker. This is important in life because it lets people know you are listening to them and helps you to concentrate better on what people say."

3. *Instructional input.* Education's recent emphasis upon the student's active role in the learning of individualized programs may have reduced teachers' confidence in the importance of formal teaching. In *Games Children Should Play*, the teacher has an active, assertive role in providing instructional input. The use of chalktalks, explanations, divergent examples, or scripts are brief but vital introductions to student response.

4. *Modeling.* Demonstrations of the skills to be attained provide examples of the desired student responses. In addition, the teacher's role as model or example needs to be sustained, from the day the teacher begins

a journal along with his or her class to the day, at the end of the school year, when the teacher joins in making a collage celebrating the accomplishments of the year.

Since communication-skills training does not take place in only an isolated time of day, but permeates the entire school day, the teacher's listening posture, use of responsible "I" messages, and problem-solving strategies provide modeling through the day to reinforce lessons.

5. *Monitor understanding.* Hunter terms monitoring a "dip-sticking" that checks the level of understanding reached by the class as a group as well as by individuals. It has been stated that the greatest problem with communication is the illusion it has been achieved. Surely the greatest problem with teaching communication skills is the illusion they have been mastered. The teacher in each lesson checks total class response as well as monitors group and individual work to answer the crucial questions: "Is this lesson appropriate to this class?" "What other skills need reinforcement in order to aid mastery of this lesson?" Student observers or referees are included in several skill practice lessons as one technique for monitoring peer understanding. On crucial concepts presented to older students, teachers can monitor understanding with individual worksheets. In the problem-solving and assertiveness chapters, student role plays provide the teacher with immediate feedback of students' understanding of the concepts being presented.

6. *Guided and independent practice.* Within the sequence of lessons, basic skills of communication are regularly reviewed to provide additional reinforcement for the student. Generally a game's format is used to capture students' enthusiasm while they practice skills of listening and speaking. Skills are then practiced intensively and reviewed as the year progresses.

7. *Reinforcement.* Reinforcement of skills is offered within each lesson as well as being recycled in subsequent lessons. At the beginning of each chapter, teachers are cued to reassess student progress and determine which, if any, lessons should be repeated before moving ahead in the sequence. Teaching for transfer involves reinforcing learned skills in other curriculum areas: praising eye contact during a social studies presentation; calling attention to clear expression during a classroom meeting; praising students' references to each other's contributions during a group discussion. When students apply newly learned communication skills to classroom and playground settings, teachers can multiply the chance of their repeating that skill by calling specific attention to it. Verbal praise or focusing peers' attention on the demonstrated skill positively reinforces the learning.

HOW TO USE THIS TEXT

This book is intended to be used with students in grades kindergarten through six, as well as with older special-education students. It is divided into two levels:

Level I: usually used with kindergarten through third-grade
  students
Level II: usually used with fourth- through sixth-grade students

Although Level I activities are written especially for primary (K–3) grade children, older groups may find those exercises appropriate as "readiness" activities for their own Level II lessons. Level I may also be used with older special-education children whose level of abstraction or ability to communicate in written fashion may necessitate more basic programming.

Lessons are arranged in sequence. The appropriate level is indicated on each lesson. Lessons without a level indication are intended for both Levels I and II.

Each chapter is introduced by clarifying which activities are essential to the strand of the continuity of the book. None of the activities within the strand should be skipped since one goal builds directly upon another. The beginning of a chapter then, clarifies which lessons are optional and may be eliminated without harming the sequence.

The book is designed to be used in one year, with lessons scheduled two or three times a week. Lessons intended for older students provide thirty to forty minutes of activity. Lessons written for younger audiences are adaptable to their far shorter attention spans. Depending upon the teacher's choice, these lessons may be as short as five minutes or as long as twenty minutes. Chapters are arranged in sequence, with listening and speaking skills preceding problem solving and assertiveness. Teachers may choose to use the lessons with the total class or in smaller instructional groups. It is convenient, but not necessary, to have a coleader when using the lessons with the total class.

Set a time limit for lessons. Avoid dragging discussions beyond the point of learning; instead leave students asking for more! It is better to continue a lesson another day than to move hurriedly through a skills training session or to teach beyond students' attention spans.

The Journal is preferably used daily, but should be used at least twice a week. The Journal clarifies current feelings, summarizes and personalizes lessons, sets goals for self-improvement.

Celebrations are scattered throughout the book. Each time, the activity is intended to be an enjoyable, entertaining celebration of skills that have been learned in earlier lessons. Further, the celebrations focus on building each child's self-image as well as fostering group cohesion and image.

Lessons appropriate to specific holiday seasons are listed in the Contents.

Short Feedback Forms at the end of the chapters provide the teacher with immediate student reaction to the lessons just completed. These feedback forms are suitable for Level II students. Activity cards will be easily used from year to year if mounted on heavy paper and laminated. Color coding by lesson or chapter helps to file them.

This text is intended for use in educational settings. As such, although activities are intended to be enjoyable, they are also educational. Emphasis is on attainment of specific objectives, not on moments of "random fun."

Activities and subject matter have been limited to those appropriate for most school settings.

Implied throughout the text is the belief that children can be bicultural; that is, they can learn ways of speaking and problem solving that are appropriate in each subculture in which they live. Students who know well the survival skills of the street can be taught the "second language" of communication skills tailored to help them adjust in school or later on a job and in the larger society. The empathetic teacher remains attuned to the pressures a child feels at home or in his or her neighborhood. Yet, too often after cataloguing the painful situations students live in, the teacher feels hopeless and helpless. The educator cannot, however, afford to let the feeling of helplessness invade education to the extent that it undermines the power of his or her teaching. Rather, the teacher can focus on the here-and-now observed needs of the child within the school setting, and make a sturdy commitment to teaching needed social skills. Again, the same principle applies to teaching communication skills as to teaching reading or math: "Find out if the child knows it, and if not, TEACH!"

It is possible to teach social behavior appropriate to a school or job setting without placing value judgments upon the behavior a student may choose to use at home or in his neighborhood. Avoiding the terms "right" and "wrong" and stressing instead "another way" or "speech suitable for school" enables the teacher to teach one model without commenting on other communication styles.

FINDING TIME TO TEACH SOCIAL SKILLS

Regardless of how convinced the teacher may be of the necessity of providing structured affective education, it is important to be able to explain to parents, administrators, and school boards, time spent in these exercises. There are at least three sources from which teachers can retrieve time to teach this program:

1. The exercises can be used in conjunction with or applied to subject matter. Each lesson is keyed to an academic subject, usually language arts and social studies, but sometimes math, art, or nutrition. Considerable emphasis is given to listening and speaking, prerequisite skills in language arts and certainly for any academic learning.

2. As every teacher knows, many moments are spent on routine tasks. Much of this time can be retrieved to create time for teaching communication skills. Using time immediately after recess or between classes for needed oral or written drills in math combinations or punctuation usage is one way of retrieving minutes.

3. Most convincing of all, add the number of minutes spent in disciplining students, battling the influence of the peer culture, and resolving individual students' problems. As a preventive guidance system, this program lays a foundation for the positive use of the peer culture and for the mutual resolution of classroom problems. It gives teacher and students a common vocabulary, and common strategies to be applied to solving new problems.

THE TEACHER'S ROLE IN AFFECTIVE EDUCATION

We view the teacher as participant as well as leader in formal affective education. By sharing feelings and ideas and thus modelling the desire to communicate, the teacher demonstrates that as Rollo May said, "therapy is life's work." When students understand that adults too have much they wish to learn about communication skills, they sense that these are life-skills.

Lessons can be adapted to any classroom structure, whether open classes or more traditional styles, so that they can be used by any teacher regardless of personal teaching style. This is a key element: the educator must feel comfortable in teaching these skills.

However, since interpersonal skills are being taught, activities emphasize one-to-one and small-group communication. By its nature, then, the course is less structured than a spelling lesson, but structured enough to be controlled and purposeful. As in any classroom activity which involves interaction, standards for behavior need to be mutually set by class and teacher. Dramatic activities, for instance, require establishing the physical limits of "the stage." Role plays also require that rules governing running and aggression be clearly set in advance. In contrast to more academic subjects, affective education demands a good deal of sensitivity on the part of the teacher. Children are encouraged to participate in each lesson, but they are not forced to do so. Their gradual attempts to contribute need to be praised. When St. Exupery's Little Prince set about to tame the fox, he came each day closer and closer to the wild and frightened animal. When teachers set about to include more withdrawn children in discussion and sharing, they need to come closer in small steps, building trust and success with each step.

In group activities, the effective teacher/leader:

1. Models a responsible stance towards his or her own feelings.
   "I'm feeling excited about this particular lesson—it teaches skills of speaking that I think we can all use."
   "I'm worried when some of you don't get a chance to speak in our small groups."
   "I was really happy when I found a game that makes sure we all get a turn."

2. Uses positive reinforcement to call attention to behavior he or she wishes to continue.
   "I am pleased that you were able to use our problem-solving method for taking care of that playground problem."
   "Did anyone notice Janie's posture when she listened to Mark?"

3. Conveys an acceptance of children's rights to have and express feelings. Avoids judging them right or wrong, appropriate or inappropriate.
   "I'm pleased that you shared with me your frustration over that misunderstanding."
   "You sound as if you're happy with that decision you made."
   "I can imagine how angry you were when that happened to you."

4. Reflects back to students their nonverbal or more hidden verbal messages. Checks to be sure the communication is sound.

   "You sound a bit unsure of that answer."

   "You nodded when John gave his idea—I'm guessing that you agreed. Is that right?"

5. Summarizes common feelings or thoughts of the group.

   "It sounds as if all of us want to plan a holiday party."

   "We all seem to be having a difficult time with this lesson. Do you think we need to try it again?"

6. Uses goal-direction statements rather than "put-downs" of student behavior.

   "I'm having a difficult time hearing Samuel when other people talk at the same time."

   "When everyone is quiet, we'll be able to start the game."

THE SCHOOL COUNSELOR OR PSYCHOLOGIST AND THIS BOOK

While counseling small groups of students is one function of pupil personnel staffs in the schools, ensuring that a greater number of students participate in preventive guidance programs is surely another function. School counselors or psychologists may increase their effect upon the school environment by using this program in one or more of these ways:

1. Working in the regular classroom with the teacher, and functioning as the second adult, or coleader, of the total classroom group during communications class time.

2. Working in the regular classroom during the scheduled communications class time, with a group of students targeted to receive counseling services based on their individual needs. (It is generally preferable to mix targeted students with those not selected by special needs so that the group includes effective models.)

3. Assuming leadership of the regular classroom's communications program, with the classroom teacher taking the role of the second adult or coleader.

4. Organizing an inservice program for teachers interested in teaching communications skills: helping them to establish the program and monitoring their classes' progress in skill attainment.

In summary, then, this text has several features as well as several limitations. It is *not*—

a system of therapy	crisis oriented
a laying-on of hands	magic
written by or for Houdinis	antiacademic
esoteric	revolutionary
risky	the last word

It *is*, however—

sequential	possible
practical	preventive
adaptable	relevant
fun	readable
inexpensive	related to curriculum
rewarding	effective
immediately useable	

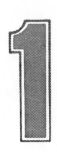

Getting Acquainted

As an introductory chapter, "Getting Acquainted" is intended to be used at the beginning of a school year, or at the initiation of this program. Several activities which will be expanded later in the year are introduced in this chapter.

"Who Am I—Today?" is an individual activity that involves each student in describing himself or herself at this particular time. As the program and school year end, this description will be compared to a then current one. Also focusing upon student growth and change, "My Own Book" (Level I) and "The Journal" (Level II) catalogue impressions and feelings on a day-to-day basis. Often, these individual books are used to summarize and personalize a directly taught lesson. The ongoing development of a class book, "ABC of Feelings" (Level I), gives children a vocabulary for and information about specific feelings.

Besides focusing in upon their own growth, this unit places students' attention upon their peers and urges their becoming better acquainted. "Who in This Class Is . . .?" (Level I) and "Be A Detective" (Level II) encourage children to find out more about each other, while "Watch the Special Person" and the "Hall of Fame" are year-long projects that spotlight positive aspects of class members and encourage positive use of the peer culture. As such, these celebrations are intended to heighten the self-images of individuals while building a sense of group pride.

STRAND (OR ESSENTIAL) LESSONS
FOR LEVEL I
(children in grades kindergarten–3 or special-education students whose maturational levels fall within that range):

Who Am I—Today?

My Own Book (a variation of The Journal)

ABC of Feelings

Who in This Class Is . . . ?

READING / WRITING / ART

WHO AM I—TODAY?
(Level I)

Goal:

To think about and describe oneself.

Materials:

Worksheet, following (readability level: grade 1.3, *Spache Readability Formula*); crayons; clear tape.

Procedure:

Focus children's thoughts upon growth and change by discussing, briefly, dramatic examples of growth: infants, puppies, kittens, seedlings. Then discuss how all people change and grow all the time. Usually this happens so slowly that we're not even aware that we are changing and growing. Ask the students if they can remember what they were like a year ago. Where were they? What did they like to do? What were they learning? Who were their friends?

Distribute the worksheet and introduce it by first reading it aloud. Tell the students that each is to put his/her name on the paper, because this, after all, is a paper about them. Direct the students to write a word to finish each sentence and to draw a picture about it, also. For students who cannot write words, either direct them to do the picture only or ask an aide or older student to write the words for them.

When the students have completed the paper, direct them to fold the sheet several times, write their name on the outside, and tape it closed. Explain that the papers will all be put away and hidden until this school year is over. At the end of the year, the children will take the papers out and read them to see how they've changed and grown.

Children enjoy the drama associated with the secrecy of the "documents." Allow some time to discuss a proper storage place for these papers.

Related Activities:

Mathematics: Measure height and weight. Include in the worksheet.

Science: Watch and measure the growth of classroom plants and pets.

WHO AM I—TODAY?
WORKSHEET—LEVEL I

My name is _____.

Today is _____.

I like to wear my _____.

WHO AM I TODAY? (Level I)

My best friend is _____.

WHO AM I TODAY? (Level I)

14

Games Children Should Play

At school I learn _____ .

I play _____ .

WHO AM I—TODAY?
(Level II)

Goal:

To think about and describe oneself.

Materials:

Worksheet, following (readability level: grade 2.2, *Spache Readability Formula*); pencils; clear tape.

Procedure:

Discuss how we change and how we grow, even though we are not always aware of our growth.

Introduce the worksheet, assuring the students that their answers will be kept secret, unless they wish to share their responses with you.

Read the questions aloud. Ask students to complete their answers in silence. Explain that when each student is finished, he/she should fold the paper into a small square, seal it with tape, and put his/her name on the outside.

Explain that at the end of the course (or school year), each student will complete another "Who Am I?" page. Students will then open the originals and compare their answers. (See exercise on page 229 for directions applicable at that time.)

Children enjoy the drama associated with the secrecy of the "documents." Allow some time to discuss a proper storage place for these "Who Am I?" worksheets.

Related Activities:

Mathematics: Measure height. Include in the worksheet.
Art: Add a self-portrait to the worksheet.

From *Games Children Should Play*,   © 1980, Mary K. Cihak and Barbara J. Heron, and Goodyear Publishing Co., Inc.

WHO AM I—TODAY?
WORKSHEET—LEVEL II

Today's date: _____   My name: _____

1. If I could choose my name, I'd be called _____.

2. My favorite color is _____.

3. My favorite television program is _____.

4. My favorite singer is _____.

5. My favorite song is _____.

6. My best friends are _____

_____.

_____.

7. My favorite game at recess is _____.

8. My favorite food is _____.

9. My favorite book is _____.

10. When I grow up, I want to be _____.

11. In school, I'm having a hard time learning _____.

12. I am afraid of _____.

13. I get angry when _____.

14. Three things I wish for: _____

_____.

_____.

15. My favorite teacher is _____.

MY OWN BOOK
(Level I)

Goals:

To develop an awareness of feelings and thoughts. To express feelings and thoughts by drawing pictures and, if possible, by writing. As the year continues, to record personal growth.

Materials:

Make a booklet for each child using twenty copies of the following worksheet; select construction paper for the covers of the books.

Background:

Much of the value of a journal lies in its regular entries. Throughout this book ideas are given for related uses of the journal. The appendix contains a list of further journal topics as well as a list of feelings. The procedure described for the first entry is intended for use on a weekly basis.

Procedure:

Introduce "My Own Book" by saying, "You each are going to make a book about yourselves. It will tell how you feel and what you are doing. It is your special book. Other people will read it only if you want them to, because it is your private book. You will write in it often. As the months go by, it will be interesting to look back and see how your feelings and thoughts have changed.

"The first thing you are going to do is to make a cover for your book. Draw a picture of yourself on the cover. Show yourself doing something that you like to do."

Introduce the first entry: "Feelings are sometimes hard to talk about. They get jumbled up inside of us. Writing about our feelings sometimes helps us understand ourselves better. Let's think a minute how we each feel right now. . . ."

Provide a model such as "Right now I'm feeling excited because you're starting to make books about yourselves. I'm going to choose to draw that feeling." Draw an oval and make an expression on the face appropriately corresponding to the feeling you mentioned.

From *Games Children Should Play*, © 1980, Mary K. Cihak and Barbara J. Heron, and Goodyear Publishing Co., Inc.

I feel _____ excited _____

because ___ you are writing a book about yourself. ___

Then draw a rectangle and show the children making their books.

Direct the students to complete their pages in a similar fashion.

MY OWN BOOK
WORKSHEET—LEVEL I

Today is _____.

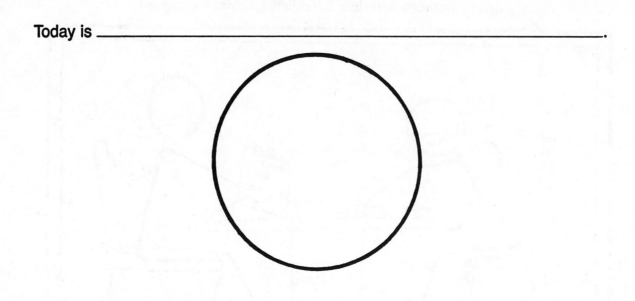

I feel _____

because _____.

Games Children Should Play

From *Games Children Should Play*,   © 1980, Mary K. Cihak and Barbara J. Heron, and Goodyear Publishing Co., Inc.

THE JOURNAL
(Level II)

Goals:

To express, in writing, personal thoughts and feelings. To provide, as the year continues, a record of growth. (In this lesson) To develop an awareness that people have ambiguous, or multiple, feelings at one time.

Materials:

Standard-sized composition notebook, preferably with lined pages, for each student and teacher.

Background:

Much of the value of a journal lies in its regular entries. Throughout this book, ideas are given for related uses of the journal. The appendix contains a list of further journal topics. The procedure described for the first entry below is intended for use on a weekly basis.

During journal-writing time, it is suggested that the teacher maintain a journal. An adult who takes time to sort out feelings and ideas provides a powerful model for children.

The journal should be stored at school in the child's desk or storage caddy. If the student completes one book and begins another during the school year, the first book should also remain at school until the end of the year.

Procedure:

Introduce the journal: "A journal is like a diary. It is your private book of thoughts and feelings. It is not meant to be shared with anyone—not with teachers, parents, or other students. Sometimes, though, you may want to invite someone to read a page of your journal.

We will be able to write in our journals regularly. As the months go by, it is interesting to look back in the journal to see how our feelings and thoughts have changed."

(Optional) Design appropriate journal covers, reflecting the interests and talents of each owner.

Introduce the first entry: "Feelings are sometimes hard to talk about. They get jumbled up inside of us. Writing about our feelings sometimes helps us understand ourselves better. Let's think for a minute about how we each feel right now. . . ."

Provide a model, such as: "Right now I'm feeling two feelings at once. I'm feeling *proud* because you did such fine work this morning; I'm feeling *excited* about starting our journals."

On the chalkboard, draw a circle divided into halves:

In each half, write one of the feelings you just discussed, repeating the reason for each one.

Ask: "What feelings are you having right now?" (Select one or two volunteers to share.)

Direct: "Open your journals to the first page, put down today's date, _____, and draw a circle divided in two parts, just as I did on the chalkboard. See if you can fill both halves of the circle."

Explain that journal writing, because it is private writing, is always done in silence.

When most are finished, add: "Now write a sentence about each feeling." (Demonstrate on board.)

I feel _____because _____.

I feel _____because _____.

Clarify: Occasionally one may have a feeling that is hard to explain. One may not know why a certain feeling occurs. Sometimes he/she may need to write: "I'm feeling _____but I don't really know why."

ALPHABET RECOGNITION / LANGUAGE ARTS / ART

A B C OF FEELINGS
(Level I)

Goals:

To increase an awareness of the variety of feelings that people have. To develop a vocabulary for describing feelings.

Materials:

Large chart paper for each letter (to be used for making a class book); large marker pen; student copy of "My Own Book" or paper; a pencil for each child.

Background:

One of the first steps in learning to deal with feelings is to be able to identify the feelings we have. Often children (and adults) are unaware of the feelings they are experiencing and therefore are blocked from dealing effectively with them. In addition to giving children a vocabulary of "feeling" words, this activity will help them to focus on specific feelings at a time when they are not likely to be overwhelmed by those feelings. In this lesson, children are helped to consider how a particular emotion feels, what kind of situation evokes it for them, and how they show it with their faces.

It is important to communicate the attitude that all feelings are acceptable. There are no right or wrong feelings. Further, it is essential that this attitude be communicated throughout the year. What is done with those feelings and how they are acted upon is the appropriate area for judgment. (Learning how to act upon feelings is dealt with in the later chapters of this book.)

Procedure:

Use the following procedure for each letter. Plan to discuss one letter a day or a week. Use a large sheet of chart paper to name and illustrate each feeling.

Discuss the letter "A", its sound and shape, how it is written. What are the feelings the students can think of that begin with the letter "A"? (angry, annoyed, anxious, astounded). Select one particular feeling for the focus of the class period. For example, if "angry" is chosen, write "A is for angry." Talk about what kinds of situations evoke the feeling of anger in the individuals in the group. Can anyone remember when he or she last felt that way? What happened to cause that feeling? How does anger feel inside? How do people look when they feel angry? Ask everyone to show with their faces how they look when they feel angry. What happens to their eyes? Mouths?

Draw a facial expression that illustrates anger under the sentence, "A is for angry." (Examples of facial expressions are on the pages that follow.) From the children's discussion, select one typical example and print a sentence under the drawing, as, "I feel angry when. . . ."

Direct the students to think about when they feel angry. Ask them then to write several examples in their "Own Book" or on other paper, "I feel angry when. . . ." If more appropriate, students may dictate their sentences to cross-age tutors, or draw pictures.

Continue with the same procedure for each letter, presenting a new letter each day or each week. (See Appendix for a list of feelings.) In later discussions, the opportunity will arise to compare feelings and to discuss shades and strengths of feelings.

Related Activities:

A lesson on cartooning or drawing faces might follow.

From *Games Children Should Play,* © 1980, Mary K. Cihak and Barbara J. Heron, and Goodyear Publishing Co., Inc.

EXAMPLES OF POSSIBLE FACIAL
EXPRESSIONS FOR "A B C OF FEELINGS"

A is for angry.

D is for discouraged.

B is for bashful.

E is for excited.

C is for curious.

F is for frustrated.

G is for glad.

J is for jolly.

H is for happy.

K is for kind.

I is for ignored.

L is for lonely.

From *Games Children Should Play*, © 1980, Mary K. Cihak and Barbara J. Heron, and Goodyear Publishing Co., Inc.

M is for mad.

N is for naughty.

O is for overwhelmed.

P is for playful.

Q is for quite silly.

R is for restless.

Games Children Should Play

S is for scared.

T is for tired.

U is for unhappy.

V is for vicious.

W is for worried.

Z is for zany.

A CELEBRATION: FAMOUS ME, THE STAR!
(Levels I and II)

Goal:

To picture oneself as competent and successful.

Materials:

A photograph of each student; art paper; drawing and coloring materials; paste; scissors.

Procedure:

Several days before you start this project, write a letter to the parents of your students telling them that you would like to have a photograph of each student for an art project that you have planned. Clarify that the picture may be cut up.

Start the project by telling the students that they are to imagine themselves as stars or famous people. They are to think about what they would be if they could be anything they wanted to be, or do anything they wanted to do. When they have an image of themselves that they really like, they are to cut out the pictures of themselves and paste them on their papers. Direct them then to illustrate the rest of the scene, showing themselves as "the great and famous me." For example, if they were a football star, they might draw the field and the other players around them, carrying them off the field on their shoulders. (If no photo is available, have them draw themselves.)

Post the pictures around the room.

Follow-up:

Direct students to write in the journals: "If I could be anything I wanted to be, I would _____."

WHO IN THIS CLASS IS . . .?
(Level I)

Goal:

To become better acquainted with the members of the class.

Procedure:

Direct students to sit in a semicircle. Call on one student to find as many people in the group who fit the category you name. Ask designated students to stand up. Then each says his or her name.

Find the people who are wearing shoes with laces in them.

Find the people who have hair that falls below their shoulders.

Find the people who have buttons on their shirts (or blouses).

Find the people who are wearing red shirts.

Find the people who are not wearing socks.

Find the people who have blue eyes.

Then ask anyone in the group to stand if he/she

has a dog at home?

likes to swim?

has a baby at home?

has an older sister? an older brother?

has been to a farm? a city?

has been to a zoo?

has ridden on a street car? an airplane? a bus?

likes to play four-square? kickball? climb on the bars?

Related Activities:

Create a bulletin board composite showing some of the questions and showing the names or self-portraits of the students who fit that category.

From *Games Children Should Play,* © 1980, Mary K. Cihak and Barbara J. Heron, and Goodyear Publishing Co., Inc.

BE A DETECTIVE
(Level II)

Goals:

To become better acquainted. To interact on a one-to-one basis within the larger group.

Materials:

Dittoed "Be a Detective" (following) for each person in class (readability level: grade 2.6, *Spache Readability Formula*).

Directions:

Give students dittoed "Be a Detective" page with instructions that they will be given ten minutes to talk to as many people as they can in order to fill in as many blanks as possible. When the signal is given (flick lights, ring bell, etc.), students are to sit down, quickly.

Discuss the findings. As individuals are named, they should stand or raise their hands to be identified.

Related Activities:

Create a bulletin board composite showing each one of the questions and the names of the students who fit in that category.

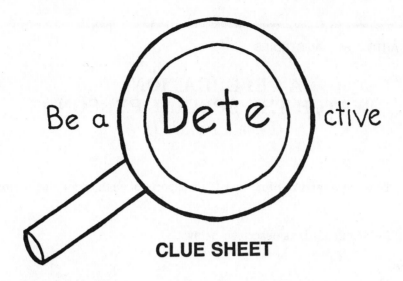

Be a Dete ctive

CLUE SHEET

Who in This Room:

Won a contest recently? _____

Had a birthday in the last two weeks? _____

Learned something new today? _____

Spent all their money on one thing this week? _____

Has an unusual pet? _____

Has lots of pets? _____

Never had a pet? _____

Likes to hold earthworms? _____

Wants to be a doctor? _____

Wants to drive a slot car more than anything else? _____

Has been to Disneyland? _____

Likes spinach? _____

Knows what a philatelist is? _____

Has a policeman for a friend? _____

BE A DETECTIVE (LEVEL II)

From *Games Children Should Play,* © 1980, Mary K. Cihak and Barbara J. Heron, and Goodyear Publishing Co., Inc.

A CELEBRATION:
WATCH THE SPECIAL PERSON
(Levels I and II)

Goal:

To observe and reinforce positive aspects of each other's behavior.

Materials:

Bulletin board, as described below.

Background:

This is a year-round celebration that focuses upon the positive behavior of students. One child is chosen by lot each week to be the Special Person. During that week, classmates watch him/her and at the end of the day report the good things they saw him/her do. This is especially effective in modifying the behavior of some individuals when they realize their good behavior gains them attention and respect from peers. You may participate as you wish in the activity.

Procedure:

Establish a bulletin board that can be used all year to highlight a different student each week. In the center of the board, place a photograph or drawing of the student with his/her name posted below the picture. Around the picture, display on cards the "good things the Special Person did." With younger children, you may need to write the cards for them during a discussion about the special person at the end of each school day. They may illustrate what good behavior they observed.

When the Special Person's week is over, he/she takes home his/her picture and the cards naming good actions done that week.

You may wish to extend the concept by closing each day with a recounting by peers of good things other students have done.

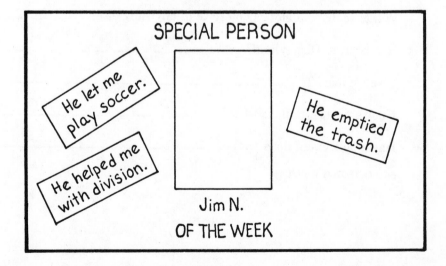

A CELEBRATION: HALL OF FAME
(Levels I and II)

Goal:

To develop pride in one's accomplishments and positive characteristics.

Materials:

Photographs of students, as described below.

Procedure:

This activity is perhaps most effective when done on a schoolwide basis throughout the year. It may, however, be produced within the single classroom.

Seek nominations from school staff members and/or from the student body of pupils who deserve recognition in the Hall of Fame. Post pictures of students, along with captions proclaiming a specific accomplishment or positive trait, in the school hallway or on classroom bulletin boards. Photos may be portraits or pictures of the honorees with their accomplishments.

Sample acclamations:

Mark knows his times tables up to the tens.

Ann plays the piano for music class.

Teresa is a volleyball star.

Carrie has read her first book.

Mary tutors younger children.

Juan learned to water ski.

Pictures and captions should be changed frequently enough for each student to be honored within the year.

FEEDBACK FORM FOR CHAPTER 1

Dear Teacher,

I _____

_____

_____

_____

_____

And furthermore, _____

_____

Sincerely,

_____

(Name)

2 Finding Out About Communication

Lessons in this chapter define clear communication as accurate listening ("receiving the message") as well as clear speaking ("getting the message across"). This two-part definition is the basis for the three chapters which follow. Therefore, it is critical that students have as good an understanding of the two components as their maturation allows. Level I students in particular may not always be able to state that communication involves sending and receiving a message; when this is the case, that definition should be reintroduced as part of the review preceding new material.

With the exception of the "The Group Story," each of the lessons in this unit is considered essential to the continuity of the program. "The Group Story" is offered as a reinforcing exercise.

LANGUAGE ARTS / SOCIAL STUDIES

COMMUNICATION: WHAT IS IT?
(Levels I and II)

Goals:

To learn a basic definition of communication. To recognize elements in clear communication.

Procedure:

Teach the word "communication." Discuss its meaning as you write on the chalkboard, "Communication involves

sending a message
and
receiving a message."

35

Emphasize that people are always communicating, sending messages and receiving messages. They do not need words to send messages. Just by the way they walk or sit or look at you they can send messages.

Ask: Can you guess what message I'm trying to send you now?

Demonstrate exaggerated facial expressions and postures, such as:

Frowning, hands on hips to communicate anger;
Smiling broadly to communicate happiness;
Eyebrows raised, arms crossed to communicate disapproval;
Hands across mouth, winking eye to communicate shared secret or shared feeling.

Discuss: Communication is not always clear. *Clear communication means that the message that one person sends is the same message the other person receives.* Clear communication requires (point to definition on board) clear messages and careful receiving. Communication is a two-way street.

Offer an example: Sometimes the message I want to send is not the one you receive. That could be because I'm not being clear, as when I can't quite get across to you how to do a math problem. Watch while I give you some mixed-up messages.

Demonstrate incongruent messages, such as:

Hands on hips, angry facial expression while saying, "I am really very happy today."
Broad smile and open posture, high voice, while saying, "I am very angry about this situation."
Pound the table and say emphatically, "I am *not* angry!"

Sometimes the message I want to send is not the one you receive because you are not receiving it carefully. I may do a good job of explaining a math problem, but you may be looking out a window or thinking of something else.

Ask for examples of times when communication is unclear.

Emphasize: Misunderstandings can happen when people *think* they have received the message clearly, but they really have not understood it. A way to be sure you have received the correct message is to ask the person who sent it.

Cite an example: I may look angry some morning and you may think I am upset with you. The only way to be sure that's why I'm looking angry is to ask me.

Choose a volunteer to participate in a brief role play in which you obviously look upset. The student asks if you are angry with him/her and you reassure the student that you are not angry at all, merely hurried as you try to get everything done.

Either read directly or organize role plays to demonstrate these sample situations. In discussing each situation, ask:

From *Games Children Should Play*,   © 1980, Mary K. Cihak and Barbara J. Heron, and Goodyear Publishing Co., Inc.

"What was the message?"
"Does this communication seem to be clear?"
"Do you think the message was sent clearly?"
"Do you think the listener listened carefully?"

The situations may lend themselves to varied interpretations. Take time to discuss the reasoning behind student responses. Encourage divergent responses as long as they are reasonable and relate to the above questions.

1 A teacher explains a math problem while the class listens carefully and understands.

2. The teacher tells a joke. One student turns to another and grins. That student smiles. (You may need to point out that communication often takes place without words.)

3. On their way home, two students pass each other in their cars. They wave.

4. Two people talk in the hall. One person shouts, "I won't do that," and walks away. The other person shrugs his shoulders.

5. A girl's little brother talks to her while she is asleep.

6. A man stops at a service station, and asks directions to Maple Street. The service station attendant says, "Oh, you go about three or four—maybe more—blocks down this way, then you turn right and a little way down that street you'll see a white house. Turn left and there's Maple Street."

7. A teenager watches a gourmet cook on television and bakes a cake according to the directions she hears. "This cake tastes different," she thinks. That night her mother says, "The cake tastes like salt. How much salt did you use?" "Two cups," says the teenager. "The cook on TV should have added sugar instead of all that salt. It would have been sweeter," the teenager says.

8. The art teacher explains how to do macramé. The students' work is beautiful.

9. Two friends have a bad argument. One friend calls the other and says, "I feel terrible about our fight. I'd like to be friends again." "I feel that way, too," says the other person. "Let's walk to school together tomorrow."

10. The quarterback tries to explain the next play to his team. Everyone runs off in different directions and the play is ruined.

11. The teacher explains long division to the class. One student is watching a softball game outside the window. When the teacher finishes the explanation and asks, "Does everyone understand?" that student shakes his head and asks for another lesson in long division.

12. A traffic cop stands directing traffic at rush hour on a busy corner. A Ford and Chevy collide.

Follow-up:

Direct students to copy from board in their journals, "Clear communication includes _____". Students write their own examples of clear and of unclear communication. Role play selected examples.

From *Games Children Should Play*,   © 1980, Mary K. Cihak and Barbara J. Heron, and Goodyear Publishing Co., Inc.

COMMUNICATION ISN'T EASY
(Levels I and II)

Goal:

To realize that both listening well and speaking clearly are difficult.

Materials:

Dittoed cards (following), one for each group of students (readability, Level I: library 2.0, lunch 2.2; Level II: 2.0; *Spache Readability Formula*).

Procedure:

Tell the students that in this version of the gossip game, some of them are going to be asked to listen to a message and to repeat it to others correctly. Elicit from the students what they can do to help themselves remember messages. Also, discuss what a person can do when telling a message in order to help another person remember it. (Emphasize speaking slowly and clearly; keeping to the essential information and not adding extraneous material.)

Divide the class into four groups. (Although it is not necessary to have an adult supervisor for each group, it is helpful.) Each group follows the same procedure:

Four students from each group are sent out of the room, with directions to be ready to listen carefully to what they are told and to be ready to repeat what they hear. The remaining students are observers. One student is called in. The group leader reads the information on the card, speaking clearly and carefully. The next student is then called in. The first student is asked to tell the report from memory to the second student. That student then reports what he/she heard to the third student. When the fourth person hears the report, he/she repeats it to the group. The observers then discuss with the group any changes they noted in the various reports.

Follow with a discussion on effective listening and speaking behavior and on ways to improve listening and speaking skills. Since this is a preliminary discussion, do not expect sophisticated or detailed responses. Use the occasion to develop interest in later lessons which will teach listening and speaking.

WHERE IS THE LIBRARY?

Yes, you can get to the library from here. Go down this hall. Then go outside. If you then go in the door on your right, you'll be in the library.

Communication Isn't Easy (Level I)

TELL ME WHERE MY LUNCH IS

I know what happened to your lunch. Listen carefully. You left it outside our classroom door. Your teacher came along and put it outside the cafeteria door. After that, Mr. Jones picked it up and put it on the steps. Ms. Kurata put it on the table in the cafeteria. I think you'll find it there.

Communication Isn't Easy (Level I)

TELL THE YARD SUPERVISOR

I was on the far part of the field when I saw what happened. The yard supervisor wants to know about it. Please tell her, because I have to go now. It is time for my class to start.

Maria and Beth were playing football. They each jumped for the ball just as Jim walked by. They bumped into each other and knocked Jim in the back. He fell down. He was angry, but he wasn't badly hurt. It really was all accidental.

Communication Isn't Easy (Level II)

THE GROUP STORY
(Levels I and II)

Goal:

To distinguish unclear communication from clear communication.

Procedure:

Ask each row or table of students to write a story together. The first student writes one sentence, folds the paper so his/her sentence does not show, and passes it on for the next student to add a sentence, etc. The "story" is then read.

DISCUSS:

"Do the stories make sense?"

"Why was this story writing NOT clear communication?"

Ask each row or table of students to write a second story. This time, the first student writes one sentence and passes it on for the next student to add a sentence, etc. The paper is not folded so that each contribution can be seen. Discuss as above.

Variation: (Level II)

Employ the above procedure, except in addition use it to reinforce the study of the parts of speech. Direct each group to write only one sentence:

The first person writes an adjective,
the second person writes a noun,
the third person writes a verb, past tense,
the fourth person writes an adverb,
the fifth person writes a prepositional phrase.

You may also reinforce elements of a composition by designating which parts of the story each person writes:

The first person writes who or what (or the subject),
the second person writes what the problem is (or the situation),
the third person writes when it happened,
the fourth person writes where it happened,
the fifth person writes the solution (or the conclusion).

From *Games Children Should Play*,   © 1980, Mary K. Cihak and Barbara J. Heron, and Goodyear Publishing Co., Inc.

FEEDBACK FORM FOR CHAPTER 2

The best part of the lesson was _____

_____.

I learned _____

_____.

I'm going to _____

_____.

_____
(Name)

FEEDBACK FORM FOR CHAPTER 2

I helped in class today by _____

_____.

Tomorrow I'm going to _____

_____.

_____
(Name)

3 Learning to Listen

"Receiving the message accurately" is a component of clear communication. Although good listening skills are basic to academic as well as social achievement, these skills often fall into the category of abilities teachers expect but do not directly teach. In this chapter, a wide variety of lessons and activities systematize the teaching of listening skills.

In "What Gets in the Way of Communication," barriers to listening are dramatized so that children see and act out the opposite of good listening. When students focus upon how it feels NOT to be listened to, they can become aware of the importance of listening to others. In other lessons, students then practice listening for content as well as for emotional tone.

Several techniques presented in this chapter are suitable for use in any discussion-oriented lesson, as in language arts or social studies classes. In particular, class meetings may be improved through the structures suggested in "Class Meetings and Observers" or "Sharing the Conversation." "Sharing the Conversation" is particularly useful in small discussion groups.

STRAND (OR ESSENTIAL) LESSONS FOR LEVEL I (children in grades kindergarten–3 or special education students whose maturational levels fall within that range):

What's That Sound?

What Gets in the Way of Communication—Part I

Nonverbal Signs of Listening

What Gets in the Way of Communication—Part II (May be too abstract for some Level I students. This lesson should be presented to Level I, but mastery not expected.)

Sharing Feelings (intended for frequent repetition during sharing time.)

Can You Hear Feelings?—Part I

42

REINFORCING LESSONS FOR LEVEL I:

Spotlight (May be a difficult concept for Level I students, and while it may be presented, mastery should not be expected.)

Sentence Building

Let's Tell a Story

STRAND (OR ESSENTIAL) LESSONS FOR LEVEL II (children in grades 4–6):

What Gets in the Way of Communication—Part I

Nonverbal Signs of Listening

What Gets in the Way of Communication—Part II

Listening Triads

Class Meetings and Observers

Spotlight

Can You Hear Feelings?—Part I

Can You Hear Feelings?—Part II

Sharing the Conversation (A technique for involving each student in small group discussions.)

REINFORCING LESSONS FOR LEVEL II:

Sentence Building

Let's Tell a Story

LANGUAGE ARTS / AUDITORY DISCRIMINATION

WHAT'S THAT SOUND?
(Level I)

Goals:

To increase awareness of environmental sounds. To develop the skill of attending.

Procedure:

Introduce the lesson by reminding children that good learners and friends are good listeners, and that this game will help them to become better listeners.

Ask children to put their heads down and close their eyes while you (or an aide) go to the back of the room and make a sound. Children who recognize the sound will raise their hands and be called upon to guess.

Suggested sounds (note: this order progresses from easiest to more difficult):

1. Clap hands	10. Stamp feet
2. Ring a bell	11. Open and shut a door
3. Blow a whistle	12. Tap a pencil on a table
4. Sneeze	13. Turn on water
5. Cough	14. Set a timer
6. Knock on the door	15. Crumple a paper
7. Play an instrument	16. Drop a pencil to the floor
(piano, drum, horn)	17. Snap fingers
8. Hum a tune	18. Sharpen a pencil
9. Hop	

Later, or on another day, seek volunteer students to go to the back of the room and make sounds while others listen and guess.

LANGUAGE ARTS / SOCIAL STUDIES

WHAT GETS IN THE WAY
OF COMMUNICATION—PART I
(Levels I and II)

Goal:

To learn the importance of listening.

Procedure:

Review the definition of communication. Stress that clear communication includes receiving the message which is sent.

Demonstrate the body language common to poor listeners. Have an adult assist you in this and in the following demonstrations, if possible. If not, select a capable student and rehearse.

Before the demonstration, instruct the class to watch carefully, and to be prepared to discuss their observations.

Demonstrate: While you speak enthusiastically (about a coming vacation or about this new unit of study), your partner obviously averts his/her eyes, yawns, turns sideways, wiggles feet, drums fingers on the desk.

Continue your attempt to communicate until most class members seem ready to respond to questions.

ASK:

"What did you see happen?"

"What was I trying to communicate?"

"Do you think ＿＿＿＿＿＿＿(the other person) really listened?"

44

Games Children Should Play

"How do you know he/she didn't listen?"

"How do you suppose I felt?"

"Do you think I would choose this person again if I wished to share with someone?"

After the discussion, a volunteer pair may be sought to demonstrate. Then, allow all students an opportunity to experience how it feels when others do not listen. Divide the class into pairs, with students taking turns being the speaker and the nonlistener.

Closing activity: As a group, take turns completing the sentence, "When people don't listen to me, I feel _____." (Note: when using open-ended sentences, children should not be made to feel embarrassed if they wish to repeat something that has already been said, or if they wish to forego their turns and "pass.")

LANGUAGE ARTS / SOCIAL STUDIES

NONVERBAL SIGNS OF LISTENING
(Levels I and II)

Goal:

To learn the nonverbal signs of attention.

Procedure:

Review with students the feelings they had when they practiced the preceding demonstrations. Write in the journals, "When people don't listen to me, I feel _____." "When I don't listen to others, they may feel _____."

Elicit students' help in making a list on the chalkboard of the body signs of good listening, such as:

Eye contact;

Squaring shoulders with the speaker (not turning to the side);

Keeping fingers and feet still;

Leaning a bit forward;

Appearing interested;

Remaining on the same level.

Select a student to demonstrate with you the body signs of listening. Exchange roles of speaker and listener. Each time, in follow-up discussion with the class, check off on the chalkboard the signs of listening which observers noted.

Divide the class into triads, groups of three, to practice these listening skills. Take turns within the triads, "A" being the speaker, "B" the listener, "C" the observer who watches for the body signs of listening.

"C" may wish to list his/her observations in a notebook. Time the practices, allowing a maximum of three to four minutes for each round before rotating roles.

SUGGESTED TOPICS:

A good dream I had.

A place I would like to visit.

My favorite food.

What I like to do after school.

What I want to be.

Follow-up:

Direct students to write in the journals, and complete the open-ended sentence, "I plan to listen better to _____, so that he/she will feel _____ ."

LANGUAGE ARTS / SOCIAL STUDIES

WHAT GETS IN THE WAY OF COMMUNICATION—PART II
(Level I, optional and Level II)

Goal:

To recognize the value of maintaining focus on the speaker and his/her topic.

Materials:

Scripts 1 and 2 (following).

Procedure:

Review the previous lessons, stressing the body language of nonlistening and of listening. Introduce Script 1: "There is more to listening than just *looking* as if you are listening. Watch this role play and see if you can decide what's wrong."

With another adult if possible, enact Script 1 or a similarly designed role play.

Discuss: "Who was the better listener?" "Why?" "How do you suppose the first speaker felt?"

Select one student who will attempt to relate something to you (about a vacation, favorite TV program, favorite food) while you divert the conversation with personal tangents.

Reemphasize that listening involves keeping the spotlight on a speaker for a reasonable time. (This concept will be explored later in more depth.)

From *Games Children Should Play,*   © 1980, Mary K. Cihak and Barbara J. Heron, and Goodyear Publishing Co., Inc.

Enact Script 2. Discuss as before.

Elicit, if possible, the generalization that communication is blocked when each person has his/her own idea in mind and does not respond to the other's ideas and feelings.

Follow-up:

Replay the scripts with good listening demonstrated.

In groups of ten to twelve, play the gossip (or telephone) game. Whisper a message to one person in each group, who then whispers it to the next, etc. Good listening is measured by how accurate the message is by the time it returns to the leader.

From *Games Children Should Play,* © 1980, Mary K. Cihak and Barbara J. Heron, and Goodyear Publishing Co., Inc.

WHAT GETS IN THE WAY OF COMMUNICATION—PART II SCRIPTS

I

(Note: As this demonstration proceeds, Speaker 1 looks more and more discouraged.)

Speaker 1:
Let me tell you about my weekend. It was so wonderful—

Speaker 2:
Oh, I had a good time on the weekend, too.

Speaker 1:
Yes, well, I've been waiting a long time for this, but I finally got to go to San Francisco. The weather was just beautiful—

Speaker 2:
I really like good weather. I can play tennis in good weather.

Speaker 1:
Good, good. Oh, I wanted to tell you about the Golden Gate bridge. It was my first experience walking across it and—

Speaker 2:
Well, you're right, I haven't had much experience with tennis. But I'm really getting better, especially with my backhand.

Speaker 1:
Yeah. I'm glad. That's nice. Anyway, in San Francisco we drove to the top of Nob Hill and we could see all over the Bay and the boats were in and—

Speaker 2:
I like boating too, but tennis is even more exciting.

Speaker 1:
Oh. Well, anyway, after that we rode down a winding little street called—

Speaker 2:
My grandmother lives on a winding street. Gee, I wish I could play tennis today.

Speaker 1:
Yeah. Well, I hope you get to play soon. So long.

II

Teacher:
We seem to have a problem on the playground.

Student:
I didn't do it.

Teacher:
You see, I don't quite know how to solve this problem.

Student:
(louder) I SAID I didn't do it.

Teacher:
We just don't have enough exercise equipment out on that playground. I wish there were a way to buy more.

Student:
I didn't—hey, did you say someone stole our exercise bars? How dare they? Wait until I get those thieves—(stalks off)

SHARING FEELINGS
(Level I)

Goals:

To recognize feelings in the facts related by others. To name those feelings one hears.

Background:

This exercise may be used any number of times, preferably during the regular sharing or show-and-tell time in the classroom. It is based upon the same technique explained in "Can You Hear Feelings—Part I," page 54, but is adapted for less mature audiences. The three response strategies explained below are listed in order of difficulty.

Procedure:

Before a student is selected to share during sharing or show-and-tell time, tell the class that they are to listen carefully and be ready to guess how that student feels about what he/she shared today.

Following a student's sharing, elicit class responses in one of the following ways:

1. Ask: "How many think _____ *(name of student)* feels happy about what he/she shared? Raise your hand if you think _____*(name)*_____ feels happy."

   (Substitute a specific feeling: proud, pleased, sad, worried, excited, etc.)

2. Ask: "Do you think _____*(name)*_____ feels glad or sad?"

   (Substitute: pleased or scared; upset or excited; happy or tired; proud or angry; etc.)

3. Ask: "What feeling do you think _____ *(name)* _____ has about what he/she shared?"

After each class response, ask the sharer if the class was accurate in its perceptions of his/her feelings.

From *Games Children Should Play*, © 1980, Mary K. Cihak and Barbara J. Heron, and Goodyear Publishing Co., Inc.

LISTENING TRIADS
(Level II)

Goal:

To refine listening skills through structured discussion.

Procedure:

Review the preceding role plays. Stress that people often do not listen to each other. They may be so busy thinking of what they want to say that they don't listen to the other person.

Explain: In this game, everyone has a chance to speak, but before each one does, he/she must repeat or summarize what the other speaker has just said to his/her satisfaction.

Demonstrate with three volunteers. While "A" and "B" converse, "C" observes and referees.

SAMPLE TOPICS:

1. Should only health foods be sold in the school cafeteria?
2. Should sixth graders have special privileges? What should they be?
3. Why would you like to be a teacher? (Or why not?)
4. Should children under ten years old be allowed to watch horror movies?
5. Should there be no-smoking sections in restaurants?
6. Should our school have a dress code?

Rotate roles in the triads, with each segment timed at three to five minutes.

Related Activity:

This technique is useful in class discussions or meetings when listening skills need emphasis. No one may state his or her idea until he or she repeats or summarizes what has been said immediately before.

From *Games Children Should Play,* © 1980, Mary K. Cihak and Barbara J. Heron, and Goodyear Publishing Co., Inc.

CLASS MEETINGS AND OBSERVERS
(Level II)

Goal:

To practice listening skills in classroom meetings or group discussions.

Procedure:

This exercise may be used whenever listening skills need improvement.

Review the body signs of good listening, listing them on the chalkboard. Discuss other signs of listening, such as asking questions of a speaker, checking to make sure you understand what the person means, or referring back to what he or she has said. Model such phrases as:

(Asking questions): "Louise, do you think that is always true?" "Can you tell us more about that?"

(Checking your understanding): "John, I hear you saying. . . . Is that what you mean?"

(Referring to someone's idea): "I agree with Dale that. . . ." "Alan, I can see your point, but I really believe that. . . ."

Divide the class into halves. One half sits as an inner circle while the other half forms an outer circle. Explain that during the discussion those in the outer circle will be looking for signs that the inner-circle discussion group is really listening to each other. (You may wish to assign each outer-circle student a specific student in the inner circle for observation. Some observers may wish to take notes.)

Direct a discussion with the inner circle, centering on concerns, subject-matter related topics, or any of the following:

"Which classroom rules are important?"

"Which school rules are important?"

"How can a new student make friends?"

"How can brothers and sisters get along with each other?"

"What kind of parent do you want to be?"

After seven to ten minutes, break to hear the observations of the outer circle. Encourage the reports to be positive in nature—ask for the signs of good listening they saw.

Reverse the circles and continue the discussion with new observers. After the discussion, each observer takes his/her partner aside and discusses what that person did well in the group and what needs improvement.

From *Games Children Should Play*, © 1980, Mary K. Cihak and Barbara J. Heron, and Goodyear Publishing Co., Inc.

Follow-up:

Direct students to write in the journals: "During the class meeting, I felt _____ because _____ ." "When I was an observer, I noticed that _____ ."

LANGUAGE ARTS / LISTENING SKILLS / GUEST SPEAKERS

SPOTLIGHT
(Levels I and II)

Goals:

To increase ability to verbally "stay with" a speaker. To learn ways to further a conversation.

Materials:

Chalkboard with possible conversation topics listed; flashlight.

Procedure:

Ask students if they know what a spotlight is. Why is it used? Tell them that this game of "Spotlight" is to help improve their listening skills. Recall with the students some of the nonlistening scripts (pp. 48–49). Discuss how it felt to be ignored or partially heard. Discuss the need to keep a conversation going between two or more people without changing the spotlight from the original speaker and topic. Elicit from them suggestions for extending questions, e.g., "How?" "What happened then?" "Why?" "What do you think?" "How did you feel?"

Now demonstrate a conversation using a flashlight to show that the "spotlight" remains on the original topic. It is preferable to have two adults demonstrate and to have a spotter who shines the spotlight (flashlight) on the original speaker as long as the conversation stays on his/her topic. If the conversation changes direction towards the other speaker or moves off the topic, the spotter turns out the light and calls "lights out." The demonstration also works well with two students who have been briefed. In that instance the teacher functions as the spotter.

Next, demonstrate a conversation using statements that change the spotlight from the original speaker to another, e.g., "That reminds me of when we . . . ," "When I . . . ," "I . . . ," "I saw . . . ," "I did it this way . . . ." The spotter calls "lights out" when these statements occur, or when the conversation fails to stay on the topic.

Now allow the group to break into triads composed of two speakers and an observer. The observer calls "lights out" if the conversation fails to stay on the original speaker and on his/her topic.

POSSIBLE TOPICS FOR TRIADS:

Last night . . . .

Next weekend . . . .

If I lived on the moon . . . .

I'd rather be the youngest (oldest, middle, only) child . . . .

This school could be improved by . . . .

My favorite lunch is . . . .

Wouldn't it be funny if . . . .

My favorite art project . . . .

A funny thing happened to me . . . .

If I could have my favorite meal . . . .

Related Activities:

This activity has an additional payoff for the classroom teacher. When a guest speaker is expected, remind the children how to keep the spotlight on the speaker. Also, when the teacher is giving directions, a comment such as "I want the spotlight on me now" will cue children to remember listening and information-gathering skills.

Further develop questioning skills by assigning interviews for the class or school newspaper.

LANGUAGE ARTS

CAN YOU HEAR FEELINGS?—PART I
(Levels I and II)

Goals:

To recognize feelings in the messages sent by others. To articulate the feelings expressed by others.

Background:

"Active listening" is the ability to hear not just the factual content but also the emotions in what people say. Further, it involves being able to give feedback to the speaker about the feelings you heard being expressed. Giving this feedback is a powerful means of checking to be certain you have understood the message clearly, that the communication has been good. Active listening techniques are elaborated in the writings of Rogers, Carkhuff, and Gordon. The exercises which follow allow students to practice the most basic active listening skills and direct reflection of feelings as they are expressed.

Procedure:

Explain that in this game listeners will not just listen to WHAT a person says; they will listen to the feelings the person communicates.

Review the nonverbal signs of good listening.

Ask students to listen to each of the following short stories and be ready to tell what feelings you are expressing.

After each short segment, ask: "What *facts* did I tell you?" "What *feelings* do you think I was telling you about?" Whenever students are unable to express the feelings adequately, explain your feelings to them. Be careful to accept divergent but appropriate responses, synonyms, or other possible feelings in each instance. Particularly in the first exercises, read very expressively to better ensure student success. If necessary, list a wide variety of feelings on the chalkboard so that students may pick appropriate ones from the list. See Appendix, "Feelings Children May Have."

1. "A terrible thing happened to me last Sunday. I had invited my best friends to come for dinner and just as I was finishing preparations for a big celebration, my phone rang. It was my friends calling. They said their car had broken down and they couldn't come after all." (Sad, disappointed, lonely, depressed, etc.)

2. "I've started a new hobby. A friend of mine showed me all about stamp collecting and now I have several books of stamps. I found out just last week that my stamp collection is worth a lot more money now than when I first bought those stamps. Besides the money the stamps are worth, I really like to look at them because they are so beautiful." (Happy, proud, secure, etc.)

3. "When I was going on summer vacation, I packed my suitcase very full of all my best clothes, my favorite books, and some nice gifts for my friends. When I got to my destination, I looked and looked for the suitcase at the airport, but I could not find it. It was lost somewhere. It had not been put on the airplane." (Angry, irritated, upset, unhappy, etc.)

4. "I saw a movie on television a few nights ago. When I started watching it I didn't know what kind of movie it was going to be. I couldn't watch until the end because I was afraid I would not have good dreams. I locked up my windows very tight that night and checked all the doors to be sure they were locked." (Afraid, uneasy, etc.)

5. "I hadn't heard from one of my nicest relatives for a long time and I was getting a bit worried about her. Last night she called to say she was feeling fine and that she would be visiting me for a day next week." (Happy, excited, etc.)

6. "Did you hear about my day yesterday? The first thing that happened was that the electricity had been off for a while so my clock was wrong, and I thought I had more time to get to school than I really did have. Then I lost my keys just as I was hurrying to get to school. When I got to school, I discovered that the substitute custodian had erased all the assignments for the day. After all that, I wondered what kind of day it was going to be. I certainly had a bad start." (Disgusted, scattered, etc.)

Select volunteers to tell briefly about an experience they have had. Ask the class: "What feeling did _____ *(name)* express?" Each time, check the accuracy of the listening by asking the speaker if that was indeed the feeling he/she had.

From *Games Children Should Play*,   © 1980, Mary K. Cihak and Barbara J. Heron, and Goodyear Publishing Co., Inc.

CAN YOU HEAR FEELINGS?—PART II
(Level II)

Goal:

To develop skills of recognizing and articulating feelings in the messages people send.

Procedure:

Review the previous lesson by asking a volunteer to tell briefly about something that happened this week. Ask students: "What feelings do you think he or she had?" Check with the speaker to be certain the communication was clear.

Divide into pairs. Designate students "A" or "B."

"A" begins, speaking on a topic assigned (list follows). Before "B" speaks, he/she must identify the feeling or feelings expressed in what "A" said. "B" begins by saying, "You're feeling . . . ." "A" confirms or denies the feeling.

Demonstrate procedure by asking one pair to model the exercise.

SAMPLE TOPICS:

My vacation;

Living with brothers and sisters;

A movie I saw recently;

Jobs I do at our house;

The time we had a substitute teacher;

How we chose which TV show to watch this week;

What I did in the game at P.E.;

What my teacher said to me today;

Getting ready for school this morning;

Learning something new;

A place I like to play;

How we decided who does what jobs at our house.

SENTENCE BUILDING
(Level II)

Goal:

To practice listening skills by focusing attention on a partner's words.

Procedure:

Students divide into pairs. Explain that each pair works together to communicate in meaningful sentences. One partner begins, saying only one word to start a sentence. Thereafter, the two students take turns, saying one word at a time. In order to make the sentences meaningful, it is important to maintain attention on what is being said.

Demonstrate with one student.

Variations:

In a small group, students converse in sentences, each person adding only one word at a time.

Add "punctuation talk" à la Victor Borge. Students agree on sounds to represent basic punctuation marks (period, comma, question mark, exclamation point) and use them in sentences as needed. Hand motions seem to follow naturally.

Example:

Students have decided the following:

PUNCTUATION MARK	SOUND
period	ppt
question mark	z z z z z z ppt
exclamation mark	w h e w w ppt
comma	sct
quotation marks	click click

THIS:

I saw Larry by the theater yesterday. I asked him, "Larry, did you like the movie?"

He replied, "It was a good movie. It was really scary!"

SOUNDS LIKE THIS:

(Pause by each needed punctuation sound.)

I saw Larry by the theater yesterday (ppt)   I asked him (sct) (click click) Larry (sct) did you like the movie (z z^z z) (click click)
z
z
ppt

He replied (sct) (click click) It was a good movie (ppt) It was really scary (') (click click)
e
w
w
ppt

LANGUAGE ARTS / SOCIAL STUDIES / DISCUSSIONS

SHARING THE CONVERSATION*
(Levels I and II)

Goals:

To increase ability to take turns speaking in a discussion group. To practice listening to others in the group.

Background:

Students not only learn to take turns with this technique, they also learn to participate in a discussion without a teacher's direction.

This technique can be used in any class discussion or in small group discussions. When the small group discussions are held simultaneously, give each group a "conversation ball."

Materials:

An old tennis ball with a face painted on it, preferably in indelible ink.

Procedure:

Introduce the "conversation ball." Tell the students that when the discussion starts, only the person holding the ball is allowed to speak. When that person is finished he/she may pass it to someone else who has his/her hand raised. The object of the game is to ensure that everyone who wants to speak gets a chance to do so.

Use a topic of your choice, or select one of the following topics:

* Adapted from *Improving Classroom Social Climate Teacher's Handbook* by Edward F. Vacha, William A. McDonald, Joan M. Coburn, and Harold E. Black. Copyright © 1977, 1979 Orcutt Union School District. Reprinted by permission of Holt, Rinehart and Winston.

Why should people learn to read?

Why should people learn to do math?

If a student wanted to raise his/her grades, what could he/she do?

Should schools sell candy? Why? Why not?

What is the best kind of class party?

How can students your age earn money?

Should you do your homework by yourself, or should your parents help you?

If you could be an animal, what animal would you be? Why?

If there weren't any schools, how would you spend your time?

If there weren't any television, how would you spend your time?

LANGUAGE ARTS / CREATIVE WRITING

LET'S TELL A STORY
(Levels I and II)

Goal:

To practice listening skills.

Materials:

Make a small yarn ball with various lengths of colored yarn. The lengths of yarn can range from about six inches to about two feet. Tie the lengths together, changing colors at each knot. Then roll the yarn into a ball. This becomes your story-telling ball.

Procedure:

Gather the students in a circle. Start a story and while you talk, rewind the ball of yarn into a new ball. When you come to a new color, pass the ball to the next person in the circle who continues the story until his/her yarn changes to a new color. The ball is then passed to the next person. As a person talks, he/she must be winding the yarn. Encourage people to listen carefully so that the story will make sense.

POSSIBLE STORY STARTERS:

Once upon a time, there was a munchkin-muffin, who lived in a lovely hole under a friendly old tree. . . .

A most exciting thing happened when Juliet and Joe were going to the park . . . .

I want to tell you about the day that I rode an elephant downtown. It all started this way . . . .

Did you ever hear about the time that J.J. got lost in a basket?

Mr. Jones was a very small worm. One day he decided to go to school and he came to this very room. He looked around and saw . . . .

From *Games Children Should Play*,   © 1980, Mary K. Cihak and Barbara J. Heron, and Goodyear Publishing Co., Inc.

FEEDBACK FORM FOR CHAPTER 3

I liked _____

_____.

I learned _____

_____.

Tomorrow I'm going to be a better listener by _____

_____.

_____
(Name)

FEEDBACK FORM FOR CHAPTER 3

I liked this lesson when you _____

_____.

One thing that would make the lesson better would be _____

_____.

I'm going to help improve the lessons by _____

_____.

_____
(Name)

4 Getting the Message Across Without Words

Some studies have estimated that as much as ninety percent of communication takes place nonverbally, without words. In this chapter, students learn that in order to receive and send messages clearly, they need to be aware of what body language—their own and other people's—communicates. They learn that messages may be sent and feelings expressed through one's posture, gestures, and facial expressions.

A variety of activities offer students practice in observing and labeling feelings that are communicated nonverbally.

Nonverbal games such as "Watch and Join Me," a group charade, provide needed practice in dramatic concentration, a prerequisite skill for later chapters which use extensive role playing.

STRAND (OR ESSENTIAL) LESSONS FOR LEVEL I:

Recognizing and Using Nonverbal Communication

Mirror Images

Who's Happy or Sad?

Show Me the Story: Checkers Game

Show Me the Story: Saturday Movie

Watch and Join Me (select five to six sequences)

REINFORCING LESSONS FOR LEVEL I:

Pictures by Pairs

Show Me the Story: Before School

Body Language

Watch and Join Me (additional sequences)

STRAND (OR ESSENTIAL) LESSONS FOR LEVEL II:

Recognizing and Using Nonverbal Communication

Mirror Images

Who Says So?

Show Me the Story: Another Move

Show Me the Story: The Vacation

Watch and Join Me (select five to six sequences)

REINFORCING LESSONS FOR LEVEL II:

Pictures by Pairs

Show Me the Story: The Ski Trip

Watch and Join Me (additional sequences)

A Celebration: Machines

A Celebration: The Picnic

RECOGNIZING AND USING NONVERBAL COMMUNICATION
(Levels I and II)

Goals:

To recognize nonverbal cues in communication. To refine nonverbal expression skills.

Materials:

Appendix: "Feelings That Children Have but Cannot Always Identify."

Background:

The following exercises may be used as a unit, or expanded into several different lessons, depending upon the group's sophistication in nonverbal communication. These exercises may also be used as warm-up drills before class discussions and meetings; they focus students' attention on the body language component of communication.

Procedure:

Review the two components of communication (listening, speaking) and discuss the progress the group has made in improving listening skills. State that not all messages are sent with words: people get messages across often without using a single word. Just by the way someone looks or stands or sits, we can know a good deal about his/her feelings and ideas.

Exercise 1: Define the term posture. Direct students to assume the following postures one at a time; ask what feeling each posture commonly conveys; ask if students have ever felt that way.

62   Games Children Should Play

Sit on edge of chair, back straight, head up.

Sit slumped down in chair, head up, legs crossed, arms folded.

Sit slumped down in chair, head down, hand on chin.

Stand, head down, shoulders slumped, arms behind back.

Stand, head erect, shoulders back, feet slightly apart, arms crossed.

Stand, feet wide apart, hands on hips.

Exercise 2: Choose individuals to demonstrate:

an angry walk;

a tired walk;

a happy walk;

a frightened walk;

a sad walk;

etc.

Use Appendix directing students to walk as if expressing one of those feelings. Observers guess the emotions being expressed.

Exercise 3: Define "facial expression." Say to the total class:

"Show me by your posture and by your facial expression (NOT by words or even by sounds) how you feel when you are:
 waiting in a dentist's office;
 waiting to give a speech in front of the class;
 in a group of much older people;
 at a football game
  when your team is winning;
  when your team is losing;
 watching an exciting TV show;
 watching a scary TV show;"
 etc.

"Show how you feel when I say;
 Recess will be ten minutes longer today;
 We'll have a big, important test tomorrow;
 I have a lot of homework for you tonight;
 I'm glad you're my class;
 I liked the way you worked this morning;"
 etc.

"Say these messages with your posture and facial expression:
 I'm happy to see you;
 I don't know;
 I'm sorry;
 I'm very angry;
 I don't care;"
 etc.

Exercise 4: Students form two teams. Each team selects one feeling from a pair of feelings the teacher writes on the chalkboard. They demonstrate that feeling nonverbally to their opponent team, as in charades. The teacher begins by suggesting very divergent feelings, such as happy/unhappy; shy/brave; then gradually closes in to more related feelings, such as hurt/angry; afraid/nervous. Variation: This exercise can be done in pairs.

At the conclusion of this lesson direct students to demonstrate to you that they can send a nonverbal message about their feelings by giving you a nonverbal message about their present feelings as they walk out of the classroom.

Related Activities: (Level I)

Include an additional exercise demonstrating opposites. Choose an individual (or a team) to demonstrate a feeling. Then ask for a volunteer (or another team) to show its opposite feeling, such as happy/sad, tired/energetic, scared/confident, brave/shy, careless/careful.

Read *Talking Without Words* by Marie Ets, Viking Press, New York.

LANGUAGE ARTS / P.E.

MIRROR IMAGES
(Levels I and II)

Goal:

To learn to receive and send nonverbal messages.

Procedure:

Review the concept of nonverbal messages. Remind the children that people are constantly sending messages with their bodies. Explain that today the students are going to practice sending nonverbal messages.

This exercise requires looking at a person and consciously reading his/her "body language." The children choose a partner. One person will be a mirror to the other. The active one is to demonstrate a variety of expressions using different postures, gestures, and facial expressions. The student who is the mirror will try to copy as closely as possible the actor's body language. First demonstrate with one student. You may want to cue some of the messages (very angry, sincere, disgusted, overwhelmed, etc. Refer to Appendix).

Change roles every one or two minutes.

Variations:

One person acts and a small group copies. One person displays an expression and maintains it. Someone in the group tries to tell what that person seems to be feeling.

Provide individual mirrors for children to look at themselves in the mirror as they change expressions.

64   Games Children Should Play

From *Games Children Should Play*,   © 1980, Mary K. Cihak and Barbara J. Heron, and Goodyear Publishing Co., Inc.

Follow-Up:

In the journal, write "I can tell how people feel by _____."
"When I feel _____, I often let people know it by _____."

Related Activities:

Movin', by Hap Palmer, Educational Activities, Inc., Freeport, N.Y. 11520. This record has appropriate P.E. activities to music: mirroring, sculpturing, acting and reacting.

LANGUAGE ARTS / SOCIAL STUDIES / ART

WHO'S HAPPY OR SAD?
(Level I)

Goal:

To increase ability to identify feelings from facial expressions.

Materials:

Magazines; collage paper; scissors; paste.

Procedure:

Post a large strip of butcher paper on a wall. Divide it into three or four vertical columns, labeling the columns as Angry, Happy, Sad, Afraid.

Read the titles of the columns with the class, asking them to demonstrate with facial expression each of the four feelings. Explain that they will be looking in magazines to find pictures of people who show each of these feelings. If necessary, demonstrate the directions by looking through a magazine, finding a face, interpreting its expression aloud, and mounting it on the paper in its proper column.

Ask students to tear or cut out the face they find that shows one of the feelings. After a student cuts out a picture, he/she is to ask one other student if he/she agrees with what the face expresses—anger, sorrow, happiness, or fear.

When two students agree, they bring the picture to be mounted. Discuss, postulating reasons for the person's feelings.

Variation: (Level II)

Follow procedure, but use feelings that may be more difficult to discriminate, such as Impatient, Discouraged, Upset, or Tired.

WHO SAYS SO?
(Level II)

Goal:

To recognize that people's facial expressions often show how they feel.

Materials:

Magazines; paste, scissors, construction paper; 3 × 5 cards; pencils.

Procedure:

Ask the students to look through magazines, cutting out pictures of faces with interesting expressions. Direct them to mount their pictures on construction paper. Next, ask them to make up something that the person in the picture could be saying, and to write the possible quotation on a 3 × 5 card.

Post the pictures and number each of them.

Mix up the quotation cards. Tack a card beside each picture. Invite the students to look at the bulletin board sometime within the week and decide whether the person in the picture is likely to be saying that posted quotation. Ask each student to write the numbers of the pictures and beside each number write a "yes" (he/she could be saying that) or "no" (he/she isn't likely to be saying that).

Follow-up:

Discuss the results of their observations.

PICTURES BY PAIRS
(Level II)

Goal:

To increase ability to communicate nonverbally.

Materials:

Sheets of large drawing paper (one for each pair of students); crayons.

Procedure:

Students are divided into pairs. Explain that each pair will cooperate to make one picture on a large sheet of art paper. No one may speak during the game. Soft music may be used as a background. Students may choose to send messages to each other on the art paper. Take time to establish

From *Games Children Should Play*, © 1980, Mary K. Cihak and Barbara J. Heron, and Goodyear Publishing Co., Inc.

ground rules for the variety of messages that may be communicated, such as: respectful, kind, friendly messages. No words may be written on the paper.

Discuss: How could one communicate "I like you" without words? (Example: heart, smile, flowers.)

After the exercise, discuss: "What messages did you try to send?" "What messages were understood?" "What messages were not understood?" "Why?"

Holiday Variation:

During the Thanksgiving season the "pictures by pairs" may illustrate the theme, "We are thankful for . . ."

SHOW ME THE STORY: THE CHECKERS GAME
(Level I)

Goals:

To practice skills of nonverbal expressiveness. To increase skills of listening for feelings.

Materials:

(Optional) Individual mirrors for each student.

Procedure:

Read the following story, pausing long enough at the dotted spaces to allow students to act out nonverbally the feelings of the leading character.

Direct students to show by their posture and facial expression the emotions related in the story.

Encourage, rather than force, participation. When necessary, directly ask for group response by saying, "How would you feel? Show me that feeling on your face."

I played checkers with my Grandpa last night. . . . I got to go over to my Grandpa's and Grandma's for dinner last night . . . all by myself! . . . Grandma fixed a special dinner for me . . . all the good things that I like to eat . . . fried chicken and mashed potatoes, yumm and . . . green beans, my favorite vegetable, and carrots, and ice cream for dessert. . . . It was a good dinner.

Then my Grandpa said he'd play a game of checkers with me. I like to play with my Grandpa, but I'd like it better if sometimes I could win. . . . We sat down and right away it seemed as if he'd taken half my checkers. . . . I hardly wanted to play anymore. . . . I decided I'd better get down to business and think about this game. . . . I looked at the

board and I watched carefully. . . . I jumped two of my Grandpa's
checkers in one play. Boy, was HE surprised. . . . He was really
surprised when I took another one of his in the next play. . . . In the end
I had two kings and he had only one. . . . I chased him around the
board. . . . I really wanted to win that game, but he's a pretty foxy player
and I was afraid that I'd still lose . . . but then I caught him . . . and I
WON THE CHECKERS GAME!

LANGUAGE ARTS

SHOW ME THE STORY:
SATURDAY MORNING
(Level I)

Goals:

To practice skill of nonverbal expressiveness. To increase skill of listening for feelings.

Materials:

(Optional) Individual mirrors for each student.

Procedure:

Read the following story, pausing long enough at the dotted spaces to allow students to act out nonverbally the feelings of the leading character.

Direct students to show by their posture and facial expression the emotions related in the story.

Encourage, rather than force, participation. When necessary, directly ask for group response by saying, "How would you feel? Show me that feeling on your face."

When I got up last Saturday morning, I thought that it was going
to be a very boring day. . . . There wasn't anything to do. . . . I was tired
of watching cartoons. . . . It seemed as though all my friends were busy
doing something else so there wasn't anybody to play with. . . . Just
when I was sure that it was going to be an awful day, Jody called me
and asked me to go to the movie . . . the one I really wanted to see.
Oh boy, I was so excited. . . . I asked my mom. . . . She looked as if
she wasn't going to let me go . . . but then she said that it was OK. . . . I
was really happy. . . . I hurried to get ready because Jody was coming
right over. . . .
I was all ready . . . except . . . I couldn't find my shoe. . . . It wasn't
under my bed . . . or anywhere in the rest of the house. . . . I just
couldn't find it anywhere. . . . I was really getting worried that I
wouldn't find it before Jody came. . . . My mom was getting upset and
said that I'd better find it because it was the second shoe I had lost in

68

Games Children Should Play

From *Games Children Should Play*,   © 1980, Mary K. Cihak and Barbara J. Heron, and Goodyear Publishing Co., Inc.

one month and money didn't grow on trees. . . . But even though she was annoyed with me, she was nice about helping me look for it. . . . Even my big brother helped me look. . . . That was a surprise! . . . I didn't think he'd help me do anything. . . . I saw Jody coming down the sidewalk and I still couldn't find my shoe. . . . Just then my brother found it for me in the dirty clothes hamper. . . . Whew, that was a relief!

Mom and my brother said good-bye and told me to have a good time. . . . I thought that was pretty nice of them after all the hard looking for my lost shoe that they did for me.

I did have a good time, too. . . . The movie was a good one, and Jody and I are even better friends.

SHOW ME THE STORY: BEFORE SCHOOL
(Level I)

Goals:

To practice skill of nonverbal expressiveness. To increase skill of listening for feelings.

Materials:

(Optional) Individual mirrors for each student.

Procedure:

Read the following story, pausing long enough at the dotted spaces to allow students to act out nonverbally the feelings of the leading character.

Direct students to show by their posture and facial expression the emotions related in the story.

Encourage, rather than force, participation. When necessary, directly ask for group response by saying, "How would you feel? Show me that feeling on your face."

Yes, I know I'm late for school. . . . Let me tell you about my terrible, awful morning. . . . The first thing that happened was that my alarm didn't go off this morning (I'm supposed to get myself up in the mornings, but I guess I forgot to set the alarm last night) so I didn't wake up. . . . Then my mother called me three times to get up, but I didn't hear her at first . . . and then I was so sleepy that I pretended to be asleep. . . . Boy, was my mother mad when she had to come wake me up! . . . Then I got upset and said that it wasn't my fault I overslept because the alarm didn't go off. . . . I hoped she would understand, but no . . . she was madder and said that I should have set it last night.

Well, I hurriedly put my clothes on, but when I got to my socks, all

From *Games Children Should Play,* © 1980, Mary K. Cihak and Barbara J. Heron, and Goodyear Publishing Co., Inc.

I could find was one red sock and one blue sock. I couldn't go to school that way! I'd die of humiliation! But my mother said if I didn't hurry up I'd have to go that way. . . . Finally I decided not to wear any socks. . . . Now my feet are cold and they are getting blisters on them.

When I got to the breakfast table everything was gone but one cold piece of toast that didn't even have any butter on it. . . . Everybody else had eaten without me. . . . It was really lonely sitting at the table eating my cold piece of toast all by myself. . . as I was finishing the last bite, I saw the school bus leaving my bus stop. . . . I grabbed my things and ran out the door yelling for it to stop and waving my hands, but the driver didn't even see me. . . . I just stood there. . . . I was feeling so discouraged that I almost started to cry.

Just then my mother came out and told me that since I missed the bus because I didn't set the alarm and because I overslept and because I didn't put my dirty clothes in the wash so I didn't have any clean socks . . . I'd have to WALK to school.

So I did walk all that L O N G way. . . . Here I am. . . . That's why I'm late.

LANGUAGE ARTS

SHOW ME THE STORY: ANOTHER MOVE!
(Level II)

Goals:

To practice skill of nonverbal expressiveness. To increase skill of listening for feelings.

Materials:

(Optional) Individual mirrors for each student.

Procedure:

Read the following story, pausing long enough at the dotted spaces to allow students to act out nonverbally the feelings of the leading character.

Direct students to show by their posture and facial expression the emotions related in the story.

Encourage, rather than force, participation. When necessary, directly ask for group response by saying, "How would you feel? Show me that feeling on your face."

It was September, and the school year had just started. You were in the _____(name)_____ grade and you really liked your class. Some of your very best friends were in the class. . . . You had fun working with them during school time . . . and lots of fun playing with them at recess and lunchtime. . . . Oh, sometimes they said kind of mean things

Games Children Should Play

about you and you didn't like that . . . but most of the time they were kind. . . . As a matter of fact, you were getting a great ball team organized. . . . You were sure your team would be better than any other team. . . . You even challenged another class to a game next week. . . . It was a good year. . . .

Then one afternoon when you were feeling really good . . . you came home and saw your mom sitting at the kitchen table. . . . She looked so concerned, it made you feel worried too. . . . She told you she had to tell you something you wouldn't like to hear. . . . Your mind raced, thinking of terrible things she might have to tell you. . . . Maybe you were in trouble . . . or someone was sick . . . or . . . "Well," she said . . . "I have been transferred to another city and we have to move." You couldn't believe it. . . . She must be kidding . . . not when everything was going so well . . . not now. . . . You looked at her sad face again and knew she wasn't kidding. . . . Now you felt really angry. . . . "I won't go, I won't go," you said . . . all the time knowing you had to go . . . you really had to go. . . . You thought of your good friends and the fun you had. . . . Why, if we go right away, you thought, I won't be able to play in the big ball game. . . . It's not fair. . . . Your mom said she knew how hard this was and she felt upset too, but that you wouldn't have to go right away. . . . It'd be a few months. . . . It probably wouldn't be until after Christmas . . . so you'd have a little while longer to stay with your friends. . . . "Besides," she said, "you do make friends easily. There'll be new friends where we're going. . . . You'll see."

And so in January you moved away. . . . It was so hard to say goodbye to your classmates. . . . Your best friend invited you to dinner and overnight that night. . . . Everybody said they'd miss you. . . . That felt good. . . . And what do you know? As soon as the moving van pulled into your new garage and you got out of the car, three children came running up. . . . "Wow, are we glad to see you! Do you like to play ball? . . . We've got this great team, but one of the players just moved and you could take that place." . . . You felt kind of shy, but they were so friendly, you felt right at home with them before long. . . . "See you at school tomorrow. I bet we're all in the same classroom, too. . . . We'll see you." You watched them as they ran off. . . . You still missed your old friends . . . but maybe one of them will write you a letter soon. . . . Besides, those new friends seemed really fine, didn't they?

From *Games Children Should Play,* © 1980, Mary K. Cihak and Barbara J. Heron, and Goodyear Publishing Co., Inc.

SHOW ME THE STORY:
THE VACATION
(Level II)

Goals:

To practice skill of nonverbal expressiveness. To increase skill of listening for feelings.

Materials:

(Optional) Individual mirrors for each student.

Procedure:

Read the following story, pausing long enough at the dotted spaces to allow students to act out nonverbally the feelings of the leading character.

Direct students to show by their posture and facial expression the emotions related in the story.

Encourage, rather than force, participation. When necessary, directly ask for group response by saying, "How would you feel? Show me that feeling on your face."

One night last May, your father said, "I think we should all go on a vacation this summer. . . . We could do something really special because my business is doing very well these days . . . and I think we should all celebrate. Make a list of all the places you want to go and we'll talk about it in a few days."

So, you thought . . . and thought . . . and made a long list of all the places you wanted to go. . . . You put Disneyland right at the top of the list . . . . It would be so much fun to be scared on the Matterhorn ride and to see the crocodiles on the Jungle Cruise. And you put the Grand Canyon on your list. . . . Everybody has said it's so beautiful you just can't believe it's real. And Washington, D.C. . . . How exciting it would be to see the White House . . . and the Congress . . . and the President.

Every day you thought of more places so you added them to your list. Then you decided to count the places you'd listed. You couldn't believe it. . . . You had a list of thirty places. . . . "Oh, oh," you thought, "Dad might not have enough time to go to thirty places." . . . But there was no harm in asking.

When the time came for discussion you brought your list. . . . It felt kind of embarrassing to have such a long list. . . . You tried to hide it behind your back. . . . What if Dad got mad because it was such a long list?

Dad said, "What's that you have there?" . . .

"Oh, nothin' important," you said, still trying to hide the list.

"I bet it's the list of places you want to see this summer," Dad said. You handed it to him to read.

"Oh, my," Dad said, "What a long list!"

72

Games Children Should Play

From *Games Children Should Play,* © 1980, Mary K. Cihak and Barbara J. Heron, and Goodyear Publishing Co., Inc.

*Oh, oh, you knew you shouldn't have made such a long list. . . .
What's he going to say now? . . . Maybe he has decided to cancel the
whole trip. . . . Maybe the business isn't doing so well anymore. . . . Dad
kept reading the list and shaking his head. . . . You got more and more
worried. . . . It looked like there wouldn't be any vacation, after all. . . .
Dad just kept reading and shaking his head. . . . He mumbled, "The
Grand Canyon. I've always wanted to see that."*

*You thought that maybe there was hope after all . . . then he
frowned and muttered something you couldn't understand. At last he
said, "This is certainly a long list, but I think we can go to about three
of the places that are close by. . . . Let's take your list and get a map of
our country and see which ones we can visit. . . . I'm really excited about
this vacation. . . . If it works out well, maybe we can go to a different
state every summer and visit lots of places on your list. . . . I'm proud
that you've learned so much as to be interested in seeing so many
worthwhile places."*

Follow-up:

Have students name all the feelings the boy/girl in the story might have
now. (Remind them not to argue with the character's right to have any
feelings, whether they be feelings of disappointment, excitement, relief,
happiness, etc. Tell them to emphasize instead the conflicting emotions
he/she may feel.)

LANGUAGE ARTS

SHOW ME THE STORY:
THE SKI TRIP
(Level II)

Goals:

To practice skill of nonverbal expressiveness. To increase skill of listening
for feelings.

Materials:

(Optional) Individual mirrors for each student.

Procedure:

Read the following story, pausing long enough at the dotted spaces to
allow students to act out nonverbally the feelings of the leading character

Direct students to show by their posture and facial expression the
emotions related in the story.

Encourage, rather than force, participation. When necessary, directly ask for group reponse by saying, "How would you feel? Show me
that feeling on your face."

From *Games Children Should Play,*   © 1980, Mary K. Cihak and Barbara J. Heron, and Goodyear Publishing Co., Inc.

It was Christmas, and you hoped you'd get new skis. . . . You'd taken one beginner's lesson at the mountains last month and did so well even the instructor said you should get skis right away. . . . You mentioned it to your folks that night and they seemed impressed . . . but maybe you didn't mention it often enough. . . . After all, they might not have realized that's really what you wanted for Christmas. . . .

You walk into the living room now and under the tree, you see a long, narrow box with your name on it. . . . That's it—skis . . . all right! . . . But you don't want to get your hopes up too high because after all, last Christmas you wanted a typewriter and they wrapped up a typing book in a big box instead. . . . Some joke. . . . For all you know, that long box could be a broom handle. . . . So you try not to give your excitement away . . . try to act aloof and cool. . . . As you open the long box and see . . . SKIS! . . . Casually you invite the whole family up to the mountains next weekend to see your performance. . . . You did just have one lesson, and that makes you a bit nervous . . . but after all, the instructor said you were a natural . . . and he should know, right?

So, it's Saturday and time to display your skiing skills on those new skis. . . . You have a little difficulty trying to remember how to get them on . . . trying not to look unsure . . . and there, they're fastened. Looking down from the top of the intermediate slope, you see your family below, waving and cheering on their hero. . . . This is the moment. . . . You put your shoulders back, hoping they look good in the new blue ski jacket . . . and slowly take off. . . . Everything is smooth. . . . What a beautiful day! . . . The air crisp, the sky blue, the trees covered with heavy snow . . . what an experience. . . . You look up slightly, straining to find your family. . . . There they are, looking so very proud. . . . You lift one pole quickly to give a humble wave to the folks when . . . a tree! . . . You're heading right into a tree. . . . What'd that instructor say to do? Fall, that must be the thing to do . . . Just fall and roll and roll. . . . Oh well . . . one last wave to the folks and its back to the bunny slope. . . . Where's that instructor when you need him? . . .

LANGUAGE ARTS

BODY LANGUAGE
(Levels I and II)

Goal:

To recognize that body postures communicate feelings.

Materials:

Worksheet for each student (following); scissors; paste; one 12 × 18 sheet of paper.

Games Children Should Play

Procedure:

Select one student as a volunteer to demonstrate. Hold a sheet of paper before the volunteer student's face so that only his/her body is visible to the other class members. Whisper an emotion (happy, sad, mad) to the volunteer. Direct this demonstrator to show that feeling with his/her whole body. Ask the other class members to look at the student's body and to guess how he/she is feeling. Ask them to predict what expression is on the student's face. Again direct the volunteer to express the feeling with his/her whole body, then remove the paper. Discuss what feeling was projected by the student. Continue with the demonstration showing two or three contrasting feelings.

Distribute a worksheet to each student. Direct the class to look at the bodies in each picture. What might each person be feeling if he/she were holding his/her body that way? Direct the students to stand and try to put their bodies in that position. Ask them to think about how that posture *feels*. What happens to their faces? What might they be feeling inside if they were standing that way?

Direct the students to select the face that best expresses how the person in the picture is feeling. Paste it on the body. As the students complete the task, discuss the completed pictures. (You may wish to teach the word "congruent" meaning most harmonious, or in the same mood. "Which face is most congruent with the body posture?") What feelings might that person be having? What feelings is that person least likely to be experiencing? Accept divergent responses which the student can explain.

Variation: (Level II)

Cut the faces from the worksheet before duplicating it. After a discussion of body posture, teach a lesson about cartooning faces and direct the students to draw cartoon faces for each body, directing them to express feelings congruent with the posture.

BODY LANGUAGE WORKSHEET

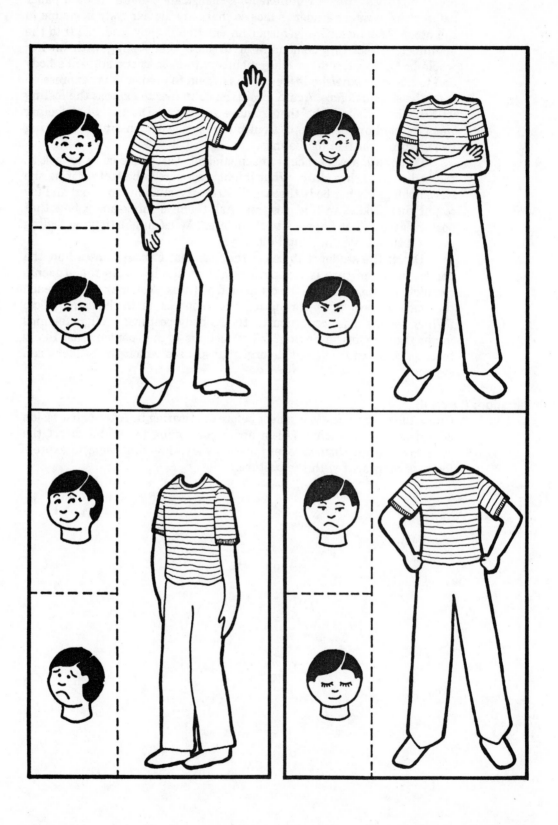

Games Children Should Play

WATCH AND JOIN ME
(Levels I and II)

Goals:

To develop skills of observation. To communicate clearly through body language.

Materials:

Task cards (following); cut and, if desired, mounted on light cardboard.

Procedure:

Seat students in rows, rather than in a circle.

Explain that one must watch carefully to understand body language, and that this skill needs practice.

Give the following directions: One student will be given a task card which describes an action. He/she goes to the front of the classroom, and begins that action. No words or sounds are allowed; only gestures are permitted, as in charades. The audience must also be silent. When someone in the audience knows what action is being done and wishes to join the actor in the charade, he/she raises a hand. The teacher beckons the child for a whispered conference. If the child has in fact recognized the action, the teacher allows him/her to join. Continue the charade as long as the action accommodates new actors. Most tasks accommodate three or four children.

Play at the park.

Watch and Join Me (Level I)   A

Learn to swim.

B

Play four-square.

C

Play tag.

D

Make lunch.

E

Games Children Should Play

Buy something at a store.

Watch and Join Me (Level I)

F

Make a bed.

Watch and Join Me (Level II)

A

Clean the house.

Watch and Join Me (Level II)

B

Bake a cake.

Watch and Join Me (Level II)

C

---

4 / Getting the Message Across Without Words

79

From *Games Children Should Play*, © 1980, Mary K. Cihak and Barbara J. Heron, and Goodyear Publishing Co., Inc.

Wash the car.

D

Have a picnic.

E

Go shopping.

F

Learn to ride a bike.

G

Games Children Should Play

Clean the yard.

Watch and Join Me (Level II)

H

Babysit 3 and 4 year olds.

Watch and Join Me (Level II)

I

Watch a scary movie.

Watch and Join Me (Level II)

J

Play volleyball.

Watch and Join Me (Level II)

K

Bathe a dog.

L

Go skateboarding.

M

Play a card game.

N

Feed the pets at a pet store.

O

Games Children Should Play

Put a jigsaw puzzle together.

P

Put up the Christmas tree.

Q

Decorate the Christmas tree.

R

Be Santa filling Christmas stockings.

S

Go Christmas caroling.

Watch and Join Me (Level II)

T

ART

A GROUP CELEBRATION: MACHINES
(Level II)

Goals:

To celebrate an increasing ability to work together as a group. To communicate nonverbally.

Procedure:

Divide the class into groups of five or six students. Direct each group to meet and to select a machine they wish to enact. Each person in the group plays part of the machine and makes only those noises appropriate to the machine. Demonstrate as needed.

Groups rejoin after a brief rehearsal. As each group performs, the remainder of the class attempts to identify the machine.

Related Activity:

Discuss an imaginary machine, its design and use. Students may wish to design a machine which combines the functions of two common machines (such as a washing-ironing machine) or they may wish to invent a new machine (such as a homework-writing machine).

Materials to be made available: cardboard boxes, tubes, paper, paint, staplers, glue, paper clips, possibly old bolts, washers, nuts, nails, small parts off machines and toys.

Proceed from group-designed blueprint to actuality. You may wish to have the construction take place without talking. Whether conducted as a nonverbal or a verbal exercise, clarify with students the objective of any group project: courteous, respectful communication of ideas.

Afer the construction, discuss: "How well did we work together?" "What were the signs of working together?" "What problems occurred?" "How might we work better next time?"

Follow-up:

Direct students to write in the journals: "When we were working together today, I felt _____."

FOLLOWING DIRECTIONS / LANGUAGE ARTS / NUTRITION

A GROUP CELEBRATION: THE PICNIC
(Level II)

Goals:

To communicate nonverbally. To cooperate and to follow directions. To celebrate.

Materials:

6 large paper bags	5 blunt knives	1 jar peanut butter
6 carrots	long spoon	22 small plastic
celery	paper towels	bags
cheese	8 oranges	32 small paper
64 crackers	1 jar Tang	plates
32 small cups	gallon container	6 paring knives
⅓ cup measure		vegetable brush
		small plastic pitcher

Cards (following). After cutting out these cards you may wish to paste or laminate them to 5 × 8 cards so that they may be reused.

(Readability levels: "Carrots," 2.7; "Tang," 3.1; "Oranges," 3.3; "Peanut butter," 3.4; "Celery," 3.6, "Cheese," 1.8 *(Spache Readability Formula)*.

Background:

This picnic has foods from each of the four food groups.

Children are directed to scrub carrots rather than peel them, since many nutrients are found in the skins of vegetables.

Procedure:

Gather the materials the night before the event. *Randomly* place the above picnic materials in the six paper bags. Put one directions card in each bag.

You will need to plan work areas. Groups preparing "Carrots," "Oranges," and "Celery" will need either to be by the sink or to have a pan of water each. Have the Tang prepared at the serving table. Provide for a place for the children to wash their hands.

Before the celebration, remind the students about nonverbal communication. Explain that they are going to have a celebration, but that all the preparation is done nonverbally. Elicit from them that this means that there can be no talking by anybody during the preparation time.

From *Games Children Should Play*, © 1980, Mary K. Cihak and Barbara J. Heron, and Goodyear Publishing Co., Inc.

Tell them that they will have to prepare for a picnic. They will be given paper bags with directions inside, but they will find that they don't have everything they need. They'll first have to gather the things they need for their task. Then they may proceed with their job. (REMEMBER, NO TALKING: this is nonverbal communication.)

After everything has been prepared and distributed, everyone may eat and talk and enjoy their picnic.

(This may well be the quietest hour you ever have in your classroom.)

Oranges

You are to make orange sections for 32 people. You will need:
    8 oranges
    2 knives
    6 plastic bags
    paper towels

When you have all of your materials, you may begin.
    1. Wash your hands.
    2. Wash the oranges.
    3. Wipe them dry.
    4. Cut each orange into 4 sections.
    5. Put the orange sections into plastic bags.
    6. Place the bags on the serving table.
    7. Clean up your area.

When you have finished, give this card to your teacher. Wait quietly for everyone to finish. You may draw or read.

The Picnic (Level II)

Peanut Butter

You are to make peanut butter cracker sandwiches for 32 people. You will need:
    crackers
    peanut butter
    3 blunt knives
    32 plates

When you have all of your materials, you may begin.
    1. Wash your hands.
    2. Set out 32 crackers.
    3. Spread each with peanut butter.
    4. Put a cracker on top of each.
    5. Place a cracker sandwich on each plate.
    6. Put the plates on the serving table.
    7. Clean up your area.

When you have finished, give this card to your teacher. Wait quietly for everyone to finish. You may draw or read.

The Picnic (Level II)

Celery

You are to make celery sticks for 32 people. You will need:
    celery
    2 knives
    6 plastic bags

When you have all of your materials, you may begin.
    1. Wash your hands.
    2. Wash the celery.
    3. Cut it into small sticks.
    4. Place the celery sticks into the plastic bags.
    5. Put the bags on the serving table.
    6. Clean up your area.

When you have finished, give this card to your teacher. Wait quietly for everyone to finish. You may draw or read.

The Picnic (Level II)

Cheese

You are to make cheese cubes for 32 people. You will need:
    cheese
    2 blunt knives
    4 small plastic bags

When you have all of your materials, you may begin.
    1. Wash your hands.
    2. Cut the cheese into 32 cubes.
    3. Place the cheese cubes in 4 plastic bags.
    4. Clean up your area.

When you have finished, give this card to your teacher. Wait quietly for everyone to finish. You may draw or read.

The Picnic (Level II)

Tang

You are to make enough Tang to fill the gallon container. You will need:
    a one-third-cup size measuring cup
    Tang
    water
    gallon container
    spoon
    32 cups
    small plastic pouring pitcher

When you have all of your materials, you may begin.
    1. Wash your hands.
    2. Follow the directions on the bottle of Tang. (Note that 4 quarts make 1 gallon.)
    3. When you have finished, use the small pitcher to pour 32 cups of Tang.
    4. Clean up your area.

When you are finished, give this card to your teacher. Wait quietly for everyone to finish. You may draw or read.

The Picnic (Level II)

Carrots

You are to make carrot sticks for 32 people. You will need:
        carrots
        2 knives
        vegetable brush
        6 plastic bags

When you have all of your materials, you may begin.
        1. Wash your hands.
        2. Scrub the carrots.
        3. Cut the carrots into small sticks.
        4. Place the carrot sticks in the plastic bags.
        5. Place the bags on the serving table.
        6. Clean up your area.

When you have finished, give this card to your teacher. Wait quietly for everyone to finish. You may draw or read.

The Picnic (Level II)

CRYPTOGRAM FEEDBACK FORM FOR CHAPTER 4

Send me a cryptogram using one sentence to tell me the best part of the lesson today.

Here are some symbols you may wish to use.

I   ear   friendship   carefree   happiness   fast

ant   hen

FEEDBACK FORM FOR CHAPTER 4

I want to learn to _____

_____.

I am proud of myself because I can _____

_____.

I like it when you _____

_____.

_____

(Name)

Getting the Message Across with Words

The second component of clear communication—getting the message across effectively—is introduced in this chapter. This chapter lays groundwork for advanced skills, problem solving, and assertiveness, which follow. Of particular importance are the lessons devoted to "I messages." By using the word "I" to express ownership of feelings and thoughts, students learn to assume responsibility for those feelings and thoughts and thus to avoid blaming others for what occurs.

Since clear communication involves both sending and receiving a message, continue to reinforce positively the signs you see of good listening during activities in this chapter. Although the focus of the lesson is upon speaking clearly, teachers should not diminish the attention they pay to signs of listening: eye contact, references to what the speaker said, ability to follow speaker's directions (see "Back-to-Back Puzzles," "Mouse in a Maze").

STRAND (OR ESSENTIAL) LESSONS FOR LEVEL I:

Tone of Voice Introduction

Tone of Voice Guessing Game

Tell Me How to Draw It

Mouse in a Maze (for more mature students or groups)

Do As I Say

Back-to-Back Puzzles

Say "I" Circle

Say "I"—Part I

REINFORCING LESSONS FOR LEVEL I:

What's Your Preference?

Say "I" Bulletin Board

A Celebration: What Is Special about Me?

92

LANGUAGE ARTS

TONE OF VOICE INTRODUCTION
(Levels I and II)

Goal:

To recognize that the same words may have very different meanings, depending upon the tone of voice one uses.

Procedure:

Discuss the concept "tone of voice." Elicit from the students' experience the fact that tone of voice changes the meaning of words we use.

On a chalkboard, write the following sentences one at a time. For the first one or two sentences, ask the entire class to read the words in a particular tone. (Possible tones of voice are suggested below.) For subsequent sentences, individual students say the words with as many variations as possible. Pause occasionally to discuss reasons for the varying emotions. For example, when might one say proudly, "I have a three-year-old sister"? When might the same words be said with annoyance?

SAMPLE SENTENCES:	*POSSIBLE CHANGING TONES:*
"I have a three-year-old sister."	proud; annoyed; excited; jealous; happy
"Our neighbor has a big police dog."	afraid; petrified; glad; curious

"My grandmother sent me a calculator for my birthday."

surprised; confused; excited; upset

"I'm going to be home alone tonight."

angry; pleased; worried; sad; overwhelmed; lonely

"Our class plays soccer at lunch time."

happy; left out; excited; disgusted

"My older brother is making lots of new friends."

glad; proud; ignored; jealous

Elicit other sentences from the students.

TONE OF VOICE GUESSING GAME
(Levels I and II)

Goal:

To identify the emotional content of words, without using nonverbal clues.

Procedure:

Review the units on nonverbal communication, by stressing how much communication is through posture, facial expression, and gestures. Tell the students that in this game, they will not see the person's posture or facial expressions as he/she speaks. Direct the class to listen very carefully, and from the way the words are said (the tone of voice), guess what feeling the speaker has.

Write a short phrase on the chalkboard (such as "Come here," "don't forget," "Oh, mother," "Is anyone home?").

Send one volunteer student to the back of the room. He/she reads the phrase with a specific emotion intended. (You may assign an emotional tone, or have the volunteer tell you in advance what feeling he/she will try to convey.)

Class members guess what feeling is being conveyed by the tone of voice.

WHAT'S YOUR PREFERENCE?
(Levels I and II)

Goal:

To make a choice quickly and to defend it in public.

Materials:

Make two sets of 5 × 8 cards by copying the following choices on them:

SET 1	SET 2
soccer	baseball
MacDonald's	Mr. Steak
cartoons	World of Disney
Coke	milk
T.V.	books
P.E.	recess
school lunches	homemade lunches
math	reading
winter	spring
cats	goldfish
chocolate	strawberry

Procedure:

You will need a helper for this. Each of you has a set of cards arranged in the above order.

Talk with the class about the importance of being able to make choices of one's own without depending on someone else to direct those choices. Distinguish between important decisions, which usually call for discussion with others and for gathering many facts and points of view, and personal preferences. Emphasize that choices are a matter of individual preference and one need not, indeed should not, be swayed by the group, even if he/she is the only one who likes a particular thing.

Tell the students that they are going to be asked to make some quick choices and to defend them. Have them meet in the middle of a court outside, or the middle of the room inside. You and your helper go to opposite sides of the court. On signal, you each raise your first card, calling out what is written on it. The students move quickly to the side of their choice. A group that is sluggish in making choices might be spurred on by the use of a stopwatch. Direct them to each find one other person with whom to discuss their reasons for making this choice.

Next, the opposite sides meet again in the middle. They take turns telling the group their reasons for choosing the side they did. This may be done by having one speaker at a time use a "soapbox" or by going down the line giving each person a chance to state one reason. Allow two to three minutes for each topic, then move on to the next set of choices.

Related Journal Topics:

"I find it hard to state my opinion when I _____."

"I find it easy to state my opinion when I _____."

LANGUAGE ARTS / ART / FOLLOWING DIRECTIONS / VOCABULARY DEVELOPMENT

TELL ME HOW TO DRAW IT
(Levels I and II)

Goals:

To give specific and clear directions. To work together cooperatively in small groups.

Materials:

One worksheet for each child (following); chalkboard; chalk.

Procedure:

Direct the students to form small groups of three to six persons. Distribute a worksheet for each child. Ask each student to design a face on the paper. Tell the students to keep their papers very secret so that you can't see them. When they've finished designing their faces, direct them to meet as a group and decide which face they'd like to use when they tell you how to draw a face on the board. While the groups are deciding which face to draw, you draw as many ovals on the board as there are groups.

When everyone is ready (still keeping their papers very secret), the groups take turns telling you how to reproduce the face which they have chosen. All members in a group may share in giving you the directions.

Follow-up:

Students may direct a partner in drawing a face. (In this case, duplicate twice as many worksheets as there are children so that each child has one to use for designing a face and one on which to follow directions.)

Variations: (Level I)

Obtain a flannel board. Make two sets of geometric shapes. Design one set to stick on a flannel board (Pellon works well for this). Keep the flannel board shapes. Hand the other set of shapes to a student. Direct him/her to arrange them on a sheet of paper, in any pattern or design he/she chooses. Then direct the student to tell you how to arrange your shapes on the flannel board in order to duplicate his/her design.

Variation: (Level II)

Direct the students to form small groups. One member of each group draws a noun from a hat, then returns to the group and directs the group how to draw the object, without telling them what it is they are drawing.

96

Games Children Should Play

(Possible nouns are: car, dog, truck, bike, book, rabbit.) When the directions are complete, the members of the group try to guess what noun it was they were drawing.

Holiday Variation:

Students use the same procedure as for designing the face, but instead, decorate the symbol for a holiday (Halloween, p. 99; Christmas, p. 100; Valentine's Day, p. 101).

TELL ME HOW TO DRAW IT

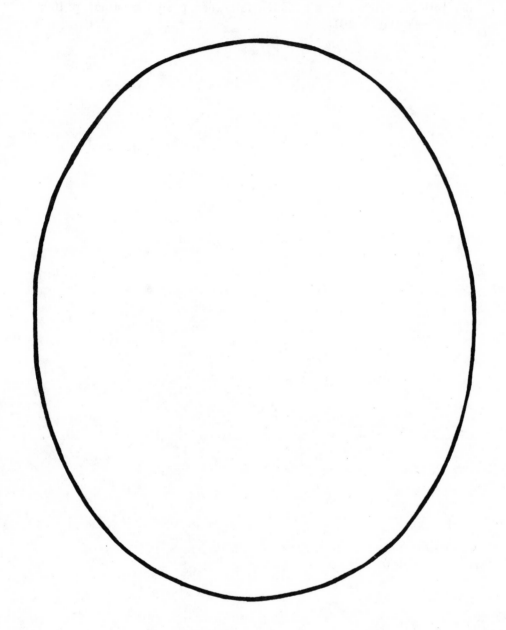

Games Children Should Play

TELL ME HOW TO DRAW IT

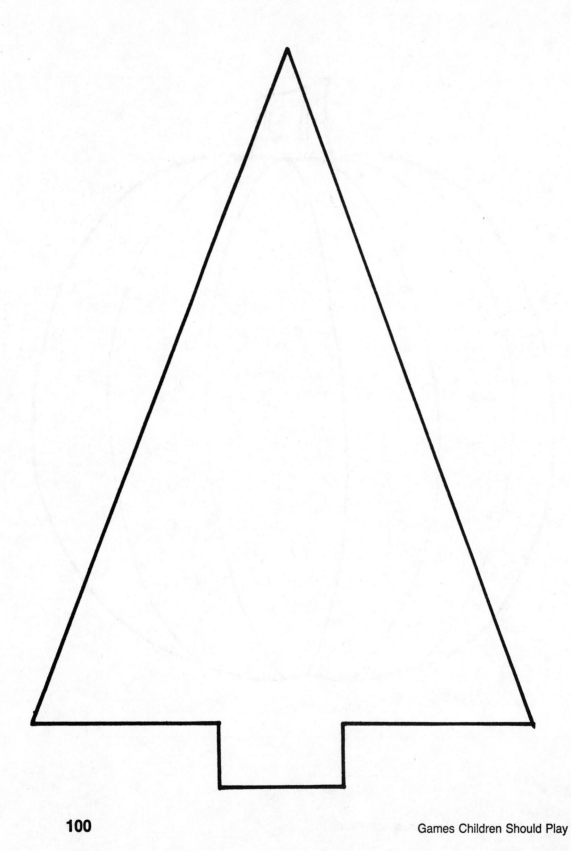

From *Games Children Should Play*, © 1980, Mary K. Cihak and Barbara J. Heron, and Goodyear Publishing Co., Inc.

TELL ME HOW TO DRAW IT

OUR OWN JACK-O'-LANTERN
(Levels I and II)

Goal:

To use specific, clear, descriptive language.

Materials:

Pumpkin; knife; candle or small flashlight; chalk; chalkboard.

Background:

This is a particularly effective exercise in helping students develop vocabulary. As students experience the need for descriptive words and as they hear adjectives and prepositional phrases from their classmates, they incorporate those words into their own vocabulary rapidly.

Procedure:

Tell the students that the pumpkin is going to become the class jack-o'-lantern. They are going to suggest ways of carving the eyes, nose, mouth for the jack-o'-lantern, and everyone will vote on each feature. You'll carve the winning features.

Ask for suggestions about how the eyes should look. Call on each student who has an idea. Direct the student to describe to you (using only words) how to make the eyes. Draw the eyes to the student's satisfaction. After all suggestions have been drawn on the chalkboard, the class then votes on the eyes they want their jack-o'-lantern to have.

Draw a pumpkin on the board and draw the chosen eyes in it.

Continue with the procedure for the nose and mouth. When the students are satisfied with their proposed jack-o'-lantern, carve it as they directed. Place a candle or flashlight in it and use it as the class mascot for the day.

LANGUAGE ARTS / GIVING DIRECTIONS / VOCABULARY DEVELOPMENT / DIRECTIONALITY

MOUSE IN A MAZE
(Levels I and II)

Goals:

To give clear directions. To follow directions.

Materials:

Several copies of the maze for each student (following) (Level I or Level II); pencils. (For follow-up: blindfold.)

Procedure:

Using a copy of the maze, decide beforehand a starting point, a path through the maze, and an ending point. Be prepared to use just words to tell students how to duplicate your path.

Tell students about experimental mice and how they are sometimes trained to go through mazes.

Give each student a copy of the maze. Direct them to find the mouse. Then, by using only words, tell them how to trace the mouse's path through the maze to the finish point. At the finish point direct them to draw some cheese. When this is completed, compare their mazes with yours. Talk about the difficulty involved in getting the message across verbally and about the importance of listening skills.

The students then form small groups. They are to take turns being leader. The leader places the cheese in the maze and plans the mouse's route. He/she then gives the group directions about where to start the mouse and how to get him to the cheese.

Follow-up:

Tell the students that one person ("mouse") will be blindfolded. He/she will have a partner who will give directions to guide him/her through a maze. The blindfolded student will try to go from one side of the room to the other without touching any of the objects in the way.

Have the "mouse" leave the room to be blindfolded. The rest of the students help set up the maze between a start and a finish line. (Chairs, books, coats, and students contribute to the maze. Be sure that there is enough space for a person to walk through the maze without touching an obstacle.) When it is ready, students may stand or sit around the perimeter of the maze, but they may not move after the game starts.

Some students may have difficulty maintaining balance and orientation when they are blindfolded. When this is the case, provide a guide who holds "mousie's" hand through the maze. Further, if the student who is giving directions has difficulty remembering "left" and "right" directionality, tape letters "L" and "R" on "mousie." "Mousie" may wish to hold something in his/her right hand in order to maintain sense of direction.

When the class is ready, "mousie" is brought to the starting line. "Mousie's" partner stands behind the finish line and directs "mousie" on how to get across the room without touching any obstacle. Score is kept on the number of touches. "Mousie" tries to get to the finish without any touches.

Related:

Literature, Mythology: Theseus and the minotaur in the labyrinth at Minos.

MOUSE IN A MAZE
WORKSHEET
(Level I)

Left   Right

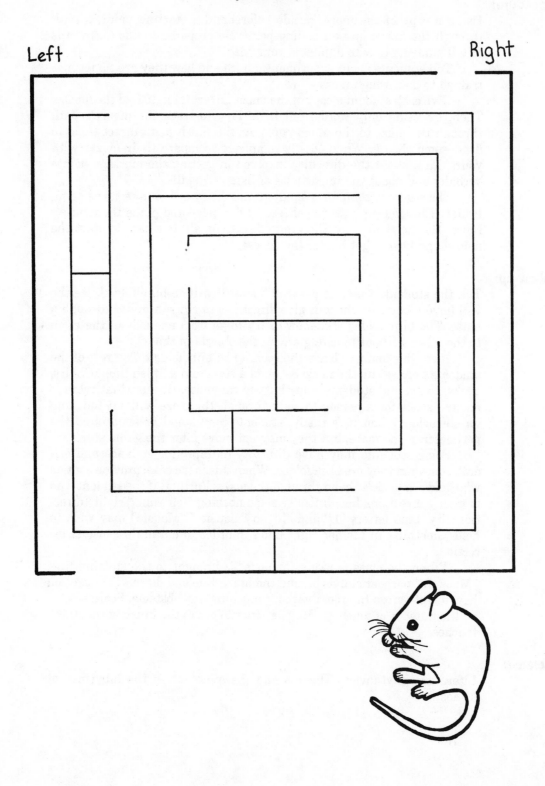

Games Children Should Play

MOUSE IN A MAZE
WORKSHEET
(Level II)

NORTH

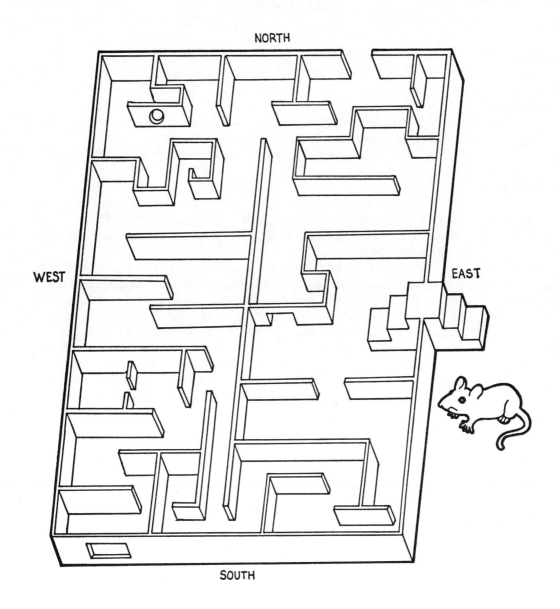

WEST

EAST

SOUTH

From *Games Children Should Play*. © 1980, Mary K. Cihak and Barbara J. Heron, and Goodyear Publishing Co., Inc.

DO AS I SAY
(Level I)

Goals:

To give specific and clear directions. To follow directions.

Materials:

Dittoed worksheet (following). (You will need one page for every four students in your class.) Cut each page into fourths.

Chalkboard space and chalk for half the number of students.

Procedure:

Distribute one card to each student. Give the students two minutes to make a design or a picture which includes or embellishes the shape on the card. Tell them to keep their pictures secret and not to show them to other people yet.

Direct the students to each find a partner, but caution them to continue to keep their pictures very secret. They are to decide who will first be the writer and who will be the speaker. The speaker will attempt to give clear enough directions to the writer that he/she can reproduce the speaker's picture on the chalkboard. The writer stands at the chalkboard with a piece of chalk. The speaker stands slightly behind the writer where the writer cannot see his/her picture, but where the speaker can see what the writer is doing at the chalkboard. When they are finished they are to compare pictures. They may then exchange roles.

DO AS I SAY
WORKSHEET

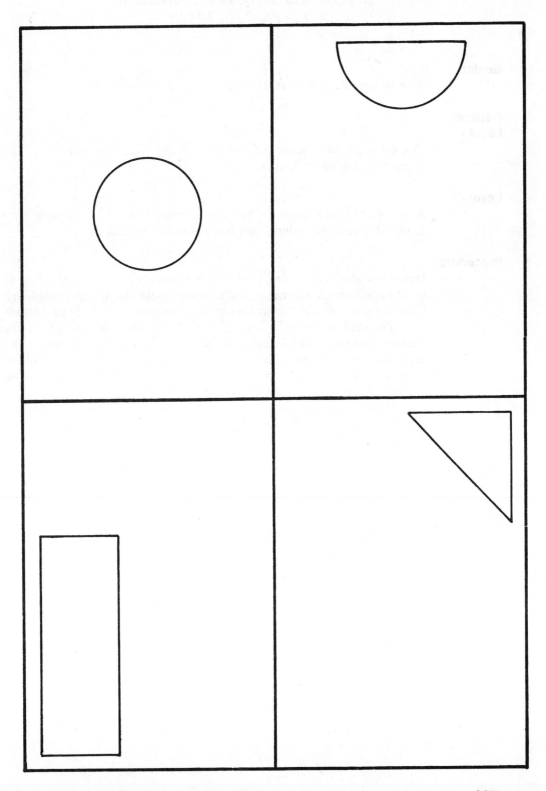

BACK-TO-BACK PUZZLES
(Levels I and II)

Goals:

To give specific and clear directions. To follow directions.

Materials
Level I:

One set of animal shapes (following); and (for second practice) one set of geometric shapes (following).

Level II:

A set of random shapes for half the number of students in your class. Each set should be unique. See one sample on worksheet.

Procedure:

Direct the students to find partners. When they have done so, they are to sit back-to-back. Give one student a card with the design pasted on it. Give the partner a blank white card and loose, duplicate design pieces.

The student with the finished design is to give directions to his/her partner about how to arrange the shapes on the blank card so that they replicate the finished design. Neither student is to look at the other's card until all the directions are given. Then they check to see how accurate they were in giving and receiving directions.

When students have put their puzzle back in the envelope, they may ask the teacher to exchange it for a new puzzle. Before accepting a puzzle for exchange, be sure to check the envelope for all the design pieces.

Follow-up:

In the journal, write "During the puzzle game, I learned _____."

Related Activity:

Divide into groups of four to five students. One student is given a picture which he/she tries to describe to the group accurately enough for each of the others to draw it.

TO THE TEACHER:
HOW TO MAKE THE PUZZLES
(Level I)

Materials:

5 × 8 cards; colored construction paper or lightweight cardboard; scissors; paste; envelopes large enough to hold the cards.

Cut out two sets of identical animal shapes from construction paper. Paste one set on a card, in random order. Place this in the envelope. Put the other set and a blank card into the envelope also.

110

TO THE TEACHER:
HOW TO MAKE THE PUZZLES
(Level II)

Materials:

5 × 8 cards; colored construction paper or lightweight cardboard; scissors; paste; envelopes large enough to hold the cards.

Cut out two sets of identical shapes from construction paper or lightweight cardboard. (Use only one color for each puzzle.) Use your imagination to create unrecognizable shapes, so that direction giving becomes a challenge. Paste one set on a card, and put into an envelope. Leave the other set loose in the envelope. Put a blank card in the envelope, also.

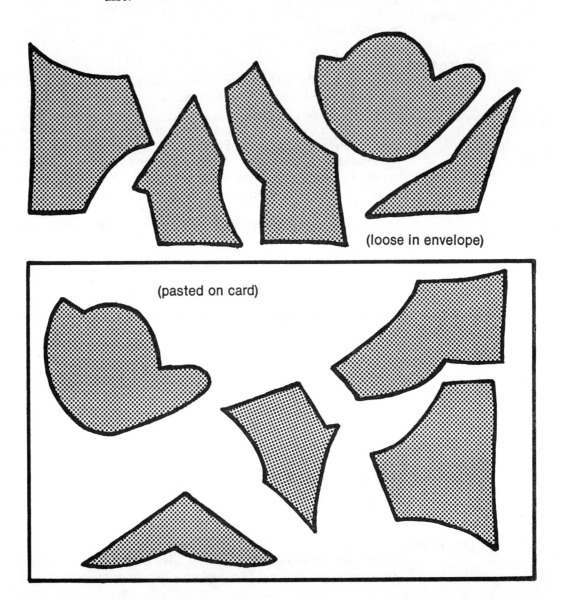

(loose in envelope)

(pasted on card)

THE DISCUSSION GAME
(Level II)

Goal:

To learn the basic principles of interaction in group discussions.

Background:

This activity is appropriate as a readiness exercise preceding classroom meetings, subject-matter discussions, or small-group buzz sessions. It requires a rehearsal with students who will aid you in the demonstrations.

Materials:

Volleyball.

Procedure:

Rehearse briefly with five volunteer students so that they will be able to follow your cues in the demonstrations. The demonstrations themselves are done without talking.

Explain to the class that the motion of the volleyball represents the flow of conversation. Remind them of the conversation ball in the lesson "Sharing the Conversation." Explain that you and the student volunteers represent members of a discussion group. Direct the class to watch carefully to see what is wrong in the discussion group when:

1. Two students toss the ball back and forth, ignoring the others.

Pause here and after subsequent illustrations to discuss what happens when similar problems are met in discussion groups. Discuss the feelings participants might have in each situation.

2. One student dribbles and then holds the ball continuously.
3. Three students toss the ball among themselves, ignoring the others' attempts to participate.
4. A designated leader directs the ball around the circle, not allowing for contributions "out of turn."
5. A designated leader tosses the ball to one student at a time, and that student always returns the ball to the leader. No member of the group tosses the ball directly to any other participant.

After the discussion of demonstration number 5, seek volunteers to demonstrate the flow of conversation in an effective group discussion. Pause periodically to praise examples of good group interaction.

Follow-up:

Divide into three discussion groups. Give a volleyball to each group with directions that they are to model an effective discussion.

A TOKEN–A TURN
(Level II)

Goal:

To contribute ideas in discussion groups.

Materials:

Paper or plastic tokens or buttons (five to seven for each student).

Background:

This exercise may be used out of sequence, and any number of times, either in curriculum-related discussions or in problem-solving sessions. While the emphasis in this exercise is on the active participation of all members of a group, encouragement of reluctant participants should be sensitive.

Procedure:

Divide the class into small discussion groups. Assign either a topic related to the curriculum or a problem for group resolution. Give each student the same number of paper or plastic tokens. Each time a student wishes to say something, he/she places one token in the center of the group. Once a student has used all of his/her tokens, that student may not contribute again until everyone's tokens have been used or until time is called.

Related Activity:

To encourage listening in class meetings, give each student two or three tokens. Students may earn additional tokens by evidencing good listening skills. Review Chapter 4 for signs of listening to be reinforced.

While you lead the discussion, an assistant walks quietly around the outside of the group circle, handing a token to individuals who display one particular good listening skill. For example, the assistant may on one occasion reinforce a student's reference to another student's contribution. On another occasion, or later in the discussion, the assistant may reinforce students who are leaning forward, looking at the speaker.

Holiday Variation:

Valentine's Day: Substitute small valentines or valentine candies for the tokens in the above Related Activity.

SAY "I" CIRCLE
(Level I)

Goal:

To identify and claim feelings, using the word "I."

Background:

This technique may be repeated frequently, varying the subjects discussed. Do not use more than three or four of the sample sentences in any one session. Form a circle for discussion, if possible including no more than ten to fifteen children. (This may be done in reading groups, or alternating groups while other children do independent written work.) It is possible to work with the entire class, but children remain more attentive when their turns to contribute come more frequently.

Procedure:

Introduce the lesson by explaining that when people speak about their feelings, they communicate more clearly when they say "I feel . . ."

Explain that in the discussion circle you will start a sentence, and anyone who wishes may complete it. Model the first sentence and others as needed. Encourage each student to participate in turn, but accept a child's desire to "pass" or to repeat something that has already been said.

SAMPLE SENTENCES (TO BE USED ON SEVERAL OCCASIONS):

1. When someone says hello to me, I feel _____.
2. When people ask me to play with them, I feel _____.
* 3. When there is a scary movie on TV, I feel _____.
4. When someone smiles at me, I feel _____.
5. When I can share with someone, I feel _____.
6. When someone shares with me, I feel _____.
7. When I get a star on my work, I feel _____.
* 8. When someone hits me, I feel _____.
9. When I get in trouble, I feel _____.
* 10. When someone likes me, I feel _____.

Gradually fade the cue "I feel" from sentences; but help students use "I feel" in their responses.

* 11. When I make a mistake, _____.
12. When I get new clothes, _____.
* 13. When I spill something on new clothes, _____.
14. When no one will let me play, _____.

15. When there's a new person in our class, _____.
16. When I'm the new person in our class, _____.
17. When I get lost, _____.
18. When I say "hello" to someone and he/she doesn't answer me, ____.
19. When someone takes my things without asking me, _____.
20. When I get dressed up to go someplace special, _____.

SAY "I"—PART I
(Level I)

Goals:

To recognize feelings. To use the word "I" to express ownership of feelings and thoughts.

Procedure:

Review the preceding lesson by stressing the need for each person to take responsibility for his/her own feelings and opinions.

Read one of the quotations which follow, then ask "How does this person feel?" After the students name some possible feelings, say, "Pretend you are this person. Tell how *you* feel. Start the sentence with the word 'I.'"

THE QUOTATIONS

1. I watched a very scary movie last night.
2. Mrs. Souza is a nice teacher. She picked me to be first in line.
3. Mother let me go shopping with her Saturday.
4. My class went on a field trip.
5. I didn't get chosen to be in the game.
6. I fell down and hurt myself.
7. Joe's mom is so mean. She won't let him play with me today!
8. This dumb jacket. The zipper is always getting stuck.
9. These are ugly shoes. The shoe laces always come untied.
10. You always get to be first in line.

SAY "I"—PART I
(Level II)

Goal:

To express responsibility for feelings and thoughts using the pronoun "I."

Background:

A critical step towards becoming responsible for one's own actions and decisions is accepting responsibility for one's feelings and thoughts. Too often individuals speak in second or third person. "You make me angry" and "Everyone is upset about the cafeteria food" are typical of language patterns which transfer responsibility from the speaker to another person. "I am becoming angry" and "I dislike the cafeteria food" are straightforward, responsible statements.

Probably the most valuable way in which children learn to say "I" is from the modeling of adults. A teacher's effort to communicate his/her feelings by speaking in the first person provides children with a powerful example.

The following lessons encourage students to own their feelings, rather than take refuge in generalizations. For the lessons to be effective, however, teachers will need repeatedly, throughout the year, to urge students to clarify their messages. The child who, in a class discussion, proclaims, "Nobody understands that silly rule" may be asked, "Who doesn't understand?" The student who insists, "That math book is too hard" may be prompted, "Do you mean, you didn't quite understand that chapter?" or "Do you mean, you would like some help with that page?"

Materials:

Two copies of script (following; readability 2.8, *Spache Readability Formula*).

Procedure:

Explain to the class that often when people speak about themselves and their own feelings, they hide by talking about someone else. For example, they will say "Everyone thinks . . ." when they mean "I think . . . ," or "Nobody likes . . ." when they mean "I don't like . . . ," or "You make me feel . . ." when they mean "I feel . . . ."

Direct the class to listen while two people (who have had a chance to rehearse) read each vignette from the script. At the end of each vignette, ask the students what the second speaker in each scene really meant. Choose a volunteer to reword the statement by beginning with the word "I."

116

Games Children Should Play

SAY "I"—PART I SCRIPTS
(Level II)

EXAMPLE

A:
I would like you to turn in your division homework.

B:
Nobody understands this assignment. It's too hard. Nobody could do it.

A:
Do you mean that you don't understand this assignment?

B:
Yes, I don't understand this assignment and I need some help on it.

1

A:
What's going on back there at that table?

B:
Make Joey stop hitting me. He's always doing something to bother me.

2

A:
I hear you didn't finish your lunch today. Is that right?

B:
Nobody likes tomatoes. Why do they keep serving tomatoes in the cafeteria?

3

A:
I noticed you haven't been participating in the reading group lately. Is anything wrong?

B:
Well, when you can't read out loud very well, you feel kind of embarrassed.

From *Games Children Should Play*, © 1980, Mary K. Cihak and Barbara J. Heron, and Goodyear Publishing Co., Inc.

4

A:
Have you had some problem with the yard supervisor?

B:
Everybody thinks he's unfair.

5

A:
How did that fight get started this morning?

B:
Well, he makes me so angry! He gets me all upset.

6

A:
You seem to be upset about something.

B:
You make me so mad because you aren't fair to people here.

7

A:
I have been wondering why you didn't want to run for class office this year.

B:
Oh, it makes me too nervous to do that.

8

A:
What would you like to do at our party?

B:
Some people like to play games.

SAY "I"—PART II
(Level II)

Goal:

To practice using the word "I" to express ownership of feelings and thoughts.

Materials:

One copy of Say "I"—Part II Worksheet (following) for each group of students (readability, 2.9, *Spache Readability Formula*).

Procedure:

Review the preceding lesson by stressing the need for each person to take responsibility for his/her own feelings and opinions.

Encourage the use of "affect" or "feeling words" when describing feelings. Often words that describe feelings are confused with phrases that tell what a person thinks, for example, "I am eager to go," or "I think that we should go," not "I feel that we should go." The clues are that "feeling words" are usually single words (see Appendix, "Feelings that Children Have But Cannot Always Identify") and "think words" are usually followed by phrases.

Divide the class into groups of no more than six students. Have each group select a secretary. Ask them to complete together the following worksheet.

When most groups have completed the task, reconvene to discuss responses. The rewritten phrases should be judged on how they communicate ownership of feelings and acceptance of responsibility. At the conclusion of the lesson, direct students to each give you an "I Message" as they leave the room.

SAY "I"—PART II, WORKSHEET

Directions: Change each of these sentences so that the speaker takes responsibility for his/her feelings.

Example: This stupid thing never works right!   I'm so frustrated because I never seem to be able to make this work!

1. He makes me so mad when he teases me!   I'm feeling _____ because he _____.

2. People get worried when they hear strange noises at night.   I get _____ when I _____.

3. The teacher makes me nervous when he talks about tests.   I feel _____ when _____.

4. It's frustrating to do fractions.   I _____.

5. You make me so upset!   I _____.

6. People irritate me when they talk about how much I've grown up!   _____.

7. It was a great day! Everyone was nice to me!   _____.

8. Sometimes my mother makes me so mad when she makes me take out the garbage!   _____.

9. People here don't play with us new kids.   _____.

10. Everyone gets upset sometime.   _____.

11. You always know the answers!   _____.

From *Games Children Should Play*,   © 1980, Mary K. Cihak and Barbara J. Heron, and Goodyear Publishing Co., Inc.

SAY "I" BULLETIN BOARD
(Levels I and II)

Goals:

To recall the importance of expressing ownership of feelings and thoughts. To make a visual reminder to say "I."

Materials:

At least one copy of the large letter "I" (following) duplicated for each student, preferably on construction paper or cardboard. A variety of materials to provide textures, i.e. sand, glitter, yarn, sandpaper, tiny plastic beads, sequins, corduroy, velvet, fur, a variety of fabric patterns, aluminum foil, wallpaper, carpet samples, etc. Glue. Scissors. Crayons.

Procedure:

Review with the students the need for taking responsibility for our own feelings and thoughts. Also, discuss why we capitalize the letter "I" when we are referring to ourselves. Using "I" is like using a name. We capitalize names and the letter "I" because we are important and our thoughts and feelings are important. They are important enough for us to take responsibility for them, to "own" them.

Distribute the letters and direct the students to decorate their letter "I" any way they choose. If there is time, they may make more than one.

When the letters have been placed on the bulletin board, tell the students that when they look at the bulletin board, it will remind them to "Say I." It will also remind them to write "I" as a capital letter when they are referring to themselves.

Variation:
(Level II)

In Level II, students could use this activity in an independent learning center.

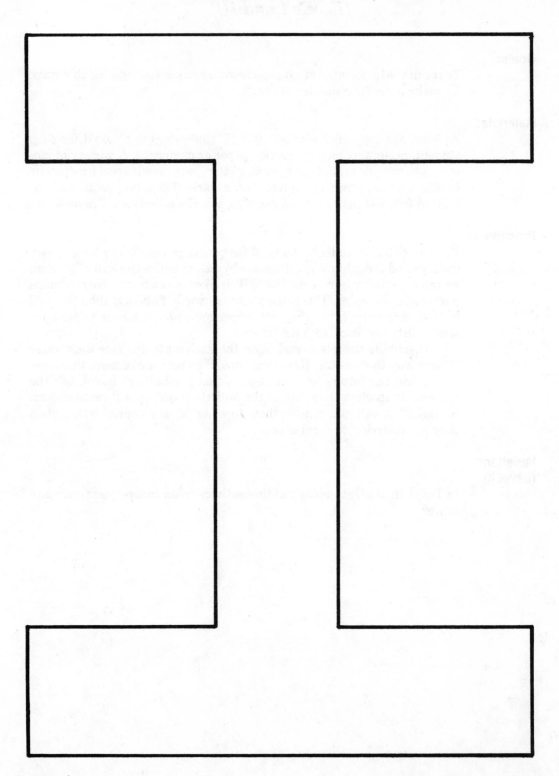

Games Children Should Play

A CELEBRATION: WHAT IS SPECIAL ABOUT ME?
(Level II)

Goals:

To become aware of one's own uniqueness. To become specific in the praise of others.

Materials:

Long sheet of paper for each student; pencils.

Background:

This activity should be done only after respect and trust have been built in the group.

Procedure:

Talk with students how how each person is unique and special. Tell the pupils that they are going to write notes telling other people in the room how they see them as special and unique. Talk about the importance of being specific. General terms such as "nice" don't really tell the person what it is we like about him/her. Specific compliments, such as "I appreciated the way you saved me a place at lunch" or "I like you because you are always fair," are more significant.

Stress that only positive things are to be written: as Thumper's father taught him, in the movie *Bambi,* "If you can't say anything nice, don't say anything at all."

Have each student write his/her name in big letters at the top of the page. Leave that paper on his/her desk. Give the students enough time to circulate through the room writing messages on each person's paper telling special things they appreciate about that person.

Be sure to put a paper out for yourself. Note also that this is an opportunity for you to give positive statements particularly to students who have problems with self-image. Be sure that no one is neglected.

Holiday Variations:

1. Valentine's Day: Draw large valentine hearts on the paper to be used.
2. Mother's Day: Invite students to make cards or posters for their mothers, listing the specific things they appreciate.

FEEDBACK FORM FOR CHAPTER 5

Today I remembered to "say I" when I said "_____

_____

_____."

I am improving my listening skills by _____

_____.

I would appreciate it if _____

_____.

I don't like it when _____

_____.

_____
(Name)

FEEDBACK FORM FOR CHAPTER 5

This lesson was best when _____

_____.

The most difficult part for me was _____

_____.

I want to improve _____

_____.

_____

(Name)

6 Solving Problems

In this unit, students apply the basic skills of listening and speaking to solving problems. These lessons in solving problems rely upon the students' ability to focus attention on their own feelings as well as on the feelings of others. Assuming responsibility for personal feelings and actions is an especially critical preliminary skill; therefore, recycling "Say 'I'" lessons may again be important.

Even within the same classroom or age group, children differ widely in their intellectual development as well as in their emotional and moral maturation. As a result, formal problem solving can be difficult even for students who functioned well in earlier Level II activities. For example, a child's thinking skills may not be developed to the point at which he or she is able to predict results of an action or to see alternatives to behavior. That type of intellectual growth cannot be forced, but it can be gently encouraged. Structured activities in this unit provide an exposure to problem solving that prompts children to look more analytically at their environment and their own behavior.

In addition to using the formal lessons, teachers can informally encourage growth in students' ability to see options for behavior and to predict consequences for each of those options.

Use events, as they happen, to teach problem solving. For example, when a child "solves" a conflict by hitting another student, the teacher may ask:

1. "What did you do?"
2. "What will happen now because of what you did?"
3. "What other way could you have solved that problem?"
4. "What would have happened if you had solved the problem that way?" (Consider each alternative.)

Help students to see alternatives to their behavior by staging role plays in which they practice other, more effective ways of solving specific problems.

126

ROLE PLAYS AND LEARNING

Another natural, informal method of encouraging growth towards problem solving is the use of role plays.

Learning activities in this chapter and in the following chapter capitalize upon children's natural gift for role playing. From their first days of "playing house," young people manage to blend naturalness with perceptive realization of the depth of problems in the larger world. Many teachers have experienced watching young stutterers play major roles in school plays without a hesitation, or seeing withdrawn preteens convincingly portray assertive roles. The magic of drama is often the magic of psychological distance. Role playing affords players the freedom to try out new roles and new solutions to problems without risking criticism of their own personal behavior or choices. Real feelings are more easily expressed when the situation is made safe by the pretense "I am really someone else today."

Through practicing many roles or different approaches to problems, children develop skills of social conduct. In this process, young people can become sensitive to feelings (their own and others'), to personal consequences of the choices they make, and to the consequences of those choices for the other people involved. Often in real life one wishes for a second chance to solve a dilemma. In role playing, the second chance is there.

Role playing is actually a group problem-solving method involving a variety of techniques:

1. Discussion;
2. Problem analysis;
3. Original enactment;
4. Observer reactions to the enactment;
5. Exploration of alternatives through further role playing;
6. Drawing conclusions or generalizations to aid in solving the problem.

As described in the general introduction, the teacher sets rules for drama sessions governing such things as running, shouting, or aggression in the role playing, as well as the physical space limits. The teacher also takes particular care to make students aware that no role player is expected to present his or her role flawlessly. The student is not evaluated for acting ability. Further, the group should be helped to understand that the way an actor portrays a role does not reflect on him or her as a person. To prevent a student's identity from being confused by the role, give actors name tags that are removed when the role is over.

While the selected role players generally prepare what they are going to do, the teacher prepares the observers to participate intelligently. Provide observers with any of the following tasks:

1. "Watch and be ready to tell us how each character feels."
2. "Watch and be ready to answer, 'Could this really happen?' "
3. "Watch and be ready to tell us what each character wants."
4. "Watch and see if you can guess what happens after this part of the role play."

The discussion following the role plays is a vital aspect of the procedure. Research has indicated that the actual taking of roles may have greatest influence on students' attitudinal change, but it is the discussion that follows the role taking that refines their problem-solving skills.

FORMAL LESSONS IN THIS CHAPTER

STRAND (OR ESSENTIAL) LESSONS FOR
LEVEL I:

Brainstorming—Students learn that there are a variety of ways to do things. This awareness and practice in discovering options paves the way for them to consider options for their own behavior as well.

What If—Students focus upon the feelings of others. This provides a basis for making decisions which affect other people.

The Pow-Wow Rug—Students learn to resolve disputes directly with the person involved rather than asking the teacher to "play judge."

What Will Happen Then?—Students consider the results of hitting, a common "solution" to peer problems. In a follow-up lesson, they learn other ways to resolve conflicts.

What Could You Do?—Students role play varied solutions to problems, taking into account each person's feelings and wants.

LEVEL II:

The lessons in problem solving are sequential. With the exception of "I'm Proud," a celebration of student achievements, each lesson is considered essential to the continuity of the program. Lessons proceed in the following order:

The Two Sides—Students recognize the basis of a problem: conflicting feelings and thoughts needing resolution.

Brainstorming—Students learn a technique that helps them discover varied possible solutions to a problem.

Seeing Consequences—Students learn to sift possible solutions, determining feasible alternatives by considering the consequences of each possibility.

The Steps in Solving Problems—Combining the above elements of problem solving, students also learn to consider the wants and feelings of persons in conflict. Role plays provide practice in the process of problem solving as well as a chance to "try out" creative problem solutions.

Once the process of solving problems is learned, problems in which the students may be "victims" are analyzed. Again, the emphasis is on personal responsibility: what can the student do to change conflicts with siblings or with peers to alter what happens to him/her? "Guess What Happens Then," "What Else Can They Do," and "What Else Can You Do" focus attention upon the "victim's" power.

THE TWO SIDES
(Level II)

Goal:

To recognize conflicting feelings and thoughts.

Materials:

Two cardboard signs, "Yes" and "No"; two chairs; script for teacher, following; worksheet for each student.

Procedure:

Initiate the lesson by asking students to draw in their journals a circle with two sections. Each section shows a feeling the student has at this time. (Review page 22.)

Discuss: Often our feelings are opposite, or mixed. We often feel two ways at the same time about one situation. For example, a student who has been benched through the class football game feels glad when his team wins, but sad that he could not be part of the game. A child may love his mother but feel angry when she restricts him.

Stress that feelings are not good or bad. It is what we do with our feelings that can be judged. What is important, first of all, is to recognize the feelings we have.

Ask students to volunteer samples of opposite feelings they have felt at the same time.

Explain: It is hard to make decisions when we have opposite feelings about a situation. Understanding that we have opposite feelings is the first step in making the decision.

Set up two chairs in front of the class. Label one the "Yes" chair, one the "No" chair.

Demonstrate the use of the chairs by appropriately moving from chair to chair as you express the feelings of "Yes" and "No" involved in a decision. A sample decision and script for your demonstration follows. Or use one of the following questions:

Should I teach a different grade next year?

Should I give the class more free time each day?

Ask for a student volunteer to demonstrate conflicting feelings involved in one of the following choices:

Should I try out for Little League?

Should I babysit to earn money?

Should I ask for a bigger allowance?

Should I do my homework right after school?

Should I tell Mom that I broke her favorite dish?

Should I tell my friend I don't want to smoke?

6 / Solving Problems

In each instance, do not strive for a solution. Make no judgments about feelings expressed. Instead, stress the ambiguity of feelings in each situation.

When the class understands the process, they may break into smaller groups to practice.

Follow-up:

Direct the students, individually or in pairs, to complete the worksheet.

Variation:

Set up the two chairs as above. Use two students, each one expressing a set of opposite feelings in the same situation.

DECISION TO BE MADE:
"Should I take money from my savings to go on vacation?"

> **In yes chair:**
> "I feel I've worked hard enough to deserve a vacation."

> **In no chair:**
> "I'm more secure when I have money in savings for an emergency."

> **In yes chair:**
> "I enjoy the culture of San Francisco—the plays and concerts, the shops."

> **In no chair:**
> "I'd feel uneasy if I didn't wait a while to get more money to go."

> **In yes chair:**
> "I know some people going now, and I will have more fun if I don't go alone."

> **In no chair:**
> "Maybe there'll be someplace else I'll want to go later, and then I won't have enough money."

> Etc.

6 / Solving Problems

131

THE TWO SIDES WORKSHEET
A DECISION I NEED TO MAKE:
(Level II)

"Should I _____?"

Yes	No

Games Children Should Play

BRAINSTORMING: SEARCH FOR SOLUTIONS
(Level I)

Goal:

To understand that there are a variety of ways to do things.

Background:

The technique of brainstorming as described in the next activity is somewhat modified for this level. Set a time limit (two to three minutes) for each brainstorming and adhere to it. Model an accepting attitude, and allow no "put downs" about any of the ideas.

Materials:

A clock or watch with a second hand.

Procedure:

Explain to the students that there are many ways of doing the same thing. In this lesson they are to suggest as many solutions to a situation as possible within the time limit you set. No negative comments or "put downs" are to be made about anyone's idea.

Select two or three topics from the following suggestions. (The remaining topics may be used for a second lesson on brainstorming or later as readiness exercises for other problem-solving sessions.)

SUGGESTED TOPICS FOR BRAINSTORMING:

1. How can you make friends with a new person at school?
2. How can you decide who will be first in a game?
3. How can you show your father or mother that you love him/her?
4. How can you help your teacher?
5. What presents can you give that don't cost money?
6. If your parents are busy, the television is broken, and you are the only child at home, what can you do by yourself to have fun?

When the time limit is up for each brainstorming topic, comment on the number of ideas submitted and the creativity shown by the students.

From *Games Children Should Play,*   © 1980, Mary K. Cihak and Barbara J. Heron, and Goodyear Publishing Co., Inc.

BRAINSTORMING: SEARCH FOR SOLUTIONS
(Level II)

Goal:

To see that there are limitless possible solutions to problems.

Background:

The well-known technique of brainstorming is intended to free the mind from its conventional paths and allow it to explore ideas that wouldn't usually be considered. Brainstorming as a step in solving problems encourages people to consider solutions that might not occur to them otherwise.

BRAINSTORMING BASICS:

1. The goal of brainstorming is to obtain as many ideas as possible. Increasing the number of and exposure to options is the objective.
2. Set a time limit and stick to it (two to three minutes).
3. Accept all ideas.
4. No "put downs" or comments about any ideas are allowed.
5. Variations of previous ideas are accepted.

Materials:

Chalkboard and chalk; eraser; a watch or clock with a second hand. It is desirable to have another adult to help record ideas.

Procedure:

Explain to the students that during a brainstorming session they will suggest as many solutions to a situation as possible within a time limit.

All ideas are acceptable.

No comments or "put downs" are to be made about the ideas.

They may use a previous idea and change it slightly.

Tell the students that they have two minutes to list all the possible uses for a ballpoint pen. They are to call out their ideas one at a time. They need not raise their hands, but they should try to take turns. The teacher writes the ideas on the chalkboard. (If another adult is available, each can write alternate ideas.)

When two minutes are up, stop and count the number of ideas the group was able to suggest. Comment positively on the number of ideas.

Suggest a second problem: "You are alone in the mountains. You have a can of food but no can opener. How many ways could you get the can open?" Allow two minutes for brainstorming the possibilities.

If desired, provide further experiences in brainstorming at a concrete level:

1. How many different means of transportation could people use to get to school?
2. How many different ways could people come into the classroom?
3. How many different ways could you use a piece of string?
4. How many different ways could you use a pocket knife?
5. How could you get across a stream that is too deep to wade, but too broad to jump?

Assure the group that now they are ready to examine a serious situation. Allow three minutes to brainstorm:

1. Ways to become friends with a new student in class.
2. What could you do to entertain yourself if the electrical power went out in your town?
3. Ways to produce a good feeling about yourself.
4. Ways to show someone you like him/her.
5. Ways of regaining the friendship of someone "mad at you."
6. How many different ways could you choose a team captain?
7. How do you assure keeping the friendship of someone who lets you pick fruit from his/her fruit tree?
8. What could you do in a talent show?

Variations:

Divide into smaller groups to provide opportunity for more students to participate. Appoint a student who can write rapidly as recorder for each group.

Have each student brainstorm his/her ideas by listing them on a piece of paper. Share the ideas at the end of the time period.

Follow-up:

Create a class collage illustrating uses for varied objects (ballpoint pen, thumbtack, paper clip).

LANGUAGE ARTS / VOCABULARY DEVELOPMENT / SOCIAL STUDIES

WHAT IF . . .
(Level I)

Goal:

To begin to develop an awareness of the feelings of others.

Background:

Level I students have only a primitive or beginning awareness of the feelings of others. Such awareness or empathy develops gradually, in keeping with children's intellectual maturation. This process involves aspects of growth that the teacher cannot force, but can encourage through experiences such as those which follow.

Try not to confine the encouragement of awareness to a formal lesson. Take advantage of opportunities to ask questions such as, "How might (name) have felt when you pushed her?" or "How do you suppose (name) will feel if you share the book with him?"

Procedure:

Review students' vocabulary of feelings by naming letters of the alphabet and seeing how many feelings the class can name for each letter or sound.

Explain that it is important for people to be able to guess how others feel at different times. Being able to guess helps people do things that start happy, not sad, feelings.

Direct students to listen as you read each story, then be ready to guess how the people in the story might feel.

SAMPLE STORIES:

1. Three people are playing ball. They won't let Mark play with them. How does Mark feel?

2. One person calls Joanne names even though Joanne asks her to stop. How might Joanne feel?

3. Judy is a new student in class. One of the children comes up to her and says, "I'm glad you're here. Would you play ball with us?" How might Judy feel? What if Judy said "No"? How might the child feel who invited her to play?

4. Wong brings a statue from home to share at sharing time. He asks that no one touch the statue, but Allen does and he breaks it. How does Wong feel? How does Allen feel?

5. Bruce made sure everyone got a turn today on the slide. How do the children feel who got a turn? How does Bruce feel? How does the person on yard duty feel?

6. Mother comes home tired from her job. Manuelito turns down the radio, gives her the newspaper, and says, "You look very tired tonight." How does mother feel now?

7. Lisa stood in line for the swings all recess and no one gave her a turn. How does she feel?

Variation:

Act out the situations as role plays, emphasizing the feelings of each character.

SEEING CONSEQUENCES
(Level II)

Goal:

To predict probable consequences to particular actions.

Materials:

Chalkboard; chalk; eraser.

Procedure:

Review the brainstorming technique. Tell the students that they are learning a technique for solving problems. After brainstorming all possible solutions, the next step is to predict the consequences that might result from each suggested solution.

Pose this problem: "You have promised a neighbor, who is ill, that you would do some work for her tomorrow afternoon. She will pay you for your work. However, a friend calls and wants you to go to the movies tomorrow afternoon."

Brainstorm possible solutions to the problem. List them in one column. Then discuss the possible consequences for each solution.

Try the procedure again with this dilemma: "You are on a committee to create a mural about your state. The others want the mural to be about the cities and industry. You want it to be about what people do for recreation in your state."

THE STEPS IN SOLVING PROBLEMS
(Level II)

Goal:

To help students understand the process of finding solutions to problems.

Materials:

Prepare a chart on which the Problem-solving Steps are written; wide chalkboard; chalk; eraser.

Procedure:

Discuss with the students the posted Problem-solving Steps. Tell them that in order to make successful choices, a person needs to be able to answer each of these questions:

From *Games Children Should Play,* © 1980, Mary K. Cihak and Barbara J. Heron, and Goodyear Publishing Co., Inc.

PROBLEM-SOLVING STEPS

1. What is the problem?
   What does each person or group want?
   How does each feel?

2. What are some ways to solve the problem?

3. What will happen when you solve the problem in each of these ways?

4. Which is the best way to solve the problem?

Pose the following situation: "Your family is going on a picnic. You want to have hamburgers to eat, but your parents want fried chicken and a salad. What can you do?"

Proceed through the Problem-solving Steps with the students:

1. List the main characters on the chalkboard. Elicit from the students what each person wants and how each feels. Write those ideas beside the characters named.

   EXAMPLE:

   Parents Want fried chicken and a salad;
            Are eager to go on a picnic;
            Want everyone to enjoy it;
            May feel nervous that there will be squabbles over the food and arrangements.

   You Want hamburgers;
         Are eager to go on a picnic;
         Want everyone to enjoy it.

2. Brainstorm ways to solve the problem. List those solutions in another column.

   EXAMPLE:

   Choice 1 Everyone could eat chicken and salad;
   Choice 2 Everyone could eat hamburgers;
   Choice 3 Parents cook their own chicken; you cook your hamburger;
   Choice 4 Have spareribs and watermelon;
   Choice 5 Go on another picnic next week, have your parents' choice one week, your choice next week;
   Choice 6 Don't go on the picnic.

3. Go over the suggested solutions and, beside each, write the probable consequences.

   EXAMPLE:

   Consequence 1 Parents satisifed with food, but unsatisfied because you don't enjoy it. You're unsatisfied with food.
   Consequence 2 You're satisfied with food, but uneasy because your parents don't enjoy it. Parents unsatisifed with food.
   Consequence 3 Both satisifed with the food.
   Consequence 4 No one may be satisfied with the food, or everyone may be satisfied with the food.
   Consequence 5 Each could be happy with compromise.
   Consequence 6 Everyone unhappy.

Games.Children Should Play

4. Choose the best way or ways to solve the problem.
   EXAMPLE:
   Choices 3, 4, and 5 appear reasonable.
5. Talk about how each person in the situation feels now.

Follow-up:

Place the "Problem–solving Steps" chart near the pow-wow rug.

ROLE PLAYS FOR PROBLEM SOLVING— PART I
(Level II)

Goal:

To practice using the process of problem solving.

Materials:

Chart of Problem-solving Steps. Ditto four or five copies of Cards A and B (following; readability level: A, 2.1; B, 2.0, *Spache Readability Formula*).

Procedure:

Review the Problem-solving Steps. Discuss the problems presented on Cards A and B using steps 1–3. Then divide the class into triads and give several groups Card A and give several Card B. Tell the groups to select a solution that seems best to them. Each group role plays their solution for the class.

You have invited a friend to your house for ice cream. Another friend calls and wants you to go to the movies. *What will you do?*

Role Plays for Problem Solving—Part I (Level II)   A

From *Games Children Should Play,* © 1980, Mary K. Cihak and Barbara J. Heron, and Goodyear Publishing Co., Inc.

Your friends and you are going to play softball. You each want to be first up to bat. How will you decide who gets to be first?

B

LANGUAGE ARTS / SOCIAL STUDIES

ROLE PLAYS FOR PROBLEM SOLVING— PART II
(Level II)

Goal:

To visualize successful solutions to problems.

Materials:

Chart of Problem-solving Steps; two or three copies each of Cards C, D, E, and F (following; readability level: C, 2.5; D, 2.5; E, 2.5; F, 2.5, *Spache Readability Formula*).

Procedure:

Review once again the Problem-solving Steps. Divide the class into triads, giving each group one of the cards. (Some groups may have the same problem.) Ask them to go through the problem-solving process and arrive at a successful solution, then prepare to role play their solution. When they are ready, have them read their problems to the class and then role play their solution.

Hint: Call on one or two groups that you expect to be most successful to perform first, so that they establish an effective model.

At the end of each role play, have the rest of the class discuss the vignette: Would the suggested solution be successful? Why? Why not? Do they have any further suggestions for the group?

Follow-up:

Have students write problems. Collect them and proofread them. Select some for class problem solving and role playing.

You are at a friend's house. You are supposed to go home now, but you are having such a good time that you don't want to go. Your friend wants you to stay. *What will you do?*

C

You and a close friend are having an especially good time together. Another person comes along and obviously wants to join you. *What will you do?*

D

You and your friends are playing on the same team in a softball game. Your best friend hits a close out. The team calls it safe, but you know it's out. *What will you do?*

E

You and a friend are at a third friend's house. The one friend wants you to leave and go swimming, leaving the third friend out. *What will you do?*

F

THE POW-WOW RUG
(Levels I and II)

Goal:

To assume a greater degree of responsibility for resolving disputes.

Background:

Earlier lessons on solving problems emphasize the individual's responsibility for resolving conflicts. This technique provides a meeting place where students can discuss and, it is hoped, solve problems they share.

Most teachers agree that their interference in solving problems between individual students is rarely effective. In fact, the adult who "plays judge" and attempts to determine who is responsible for a playground fight may merely reinforce or encourage students to blame each other or even to fight more often. By urging students to compromise and settle disputes among themselves, the adult teaches them that problem resolution is primarily their responsibility.

For students who have difficulty verbalizing their feelings, the teacher may initially guide the discussion according to patterns described on page 161.

Materials:

A small rug, placed in a corner of the room. For Level II, post the chart of Problem-solving Steps near the rug.

Procedure:

Careful teacher preparation is needed to ensure the success of this technique. Set limits for the use of the rug so that it becomes truly a problem-solving place and not an escape from lessons in progress. Before presenting the rug, answer for yourself questions such as: How will students obtain your permission to meet at the rug? Will you limit the number of students who can meet at the rug? Are spectators allowed? Can an adult oversee the dialogue? Will you set a time limit for the attempt to problem solve? In setting your limits, be aware that this technique is most often effective with two students at a time and then only if they have had a separate "cooling off time" following an argument or fight. It's all right to let an hour or more go by before providing time for problem solving.

Discuss the lessons on problem solving, calling attention to the progress students have made in taking responsibility for their feelings and trying to solve problems. Reassure students that everyone has problems, but that what is important is how they try to solve those problems. Even good friends may argue with each other; what is important is how they work to remain friends. Expressing one's own feelings and listening carefully to the other person's feelings helps one solve problems and keep friends.

From *Games Children Should Play*, © 1980, Mary K. Cihak and Barbara J. Heron, and Goodyear Publishing Co., Inc.

Explain: often students have arguments on the playground or in the class and wish to solve them without talking with anyone else. The pow-wow rug, placed in a corner of the room, can be a place where students communicate, compromise, and regain their friendship.

Present your own rules for the use of the rug.

Provide examples of how the rug may be used. Demonstrate a conversation with another adult or a student using one of the following situations. Follow the Problem-solving Steps.

1. Two students disagree with a call made at a baseball game. They argue heatedly, ending in calling each other names and making threats. When they enter the classroom, one says to the other, "I'd like to settle this by talking about it on the rug."

2. Two students argue over a pencil, each claiming it as his or hers.

3. Two students have been calling each other names. Each is feeling unhappy about it.

LANGUAGE ARTS / SOCIAL STUDIES / SEEING CONSEQUENCES / ART

WHAT WILL HAPPEN THEN?—PART I
(Level I)

Goal:

To recognize the negative consequences of trying to solve problems by hitting.

Materials:

Drawing paper and crayons for each child.

Procedure:

Keep in mind that the purpose of this lesson is *not* to elicit from the children descriptions of positive problem solving, but simply to help them understand the variety of negative consequences resulting from their attempts to solve problems by hitting. Such negative consequences may include: crying; running away; ruined friendships; ruined games; need for an adult mediator; further hitting; serious physical hurt.

Tell the students that you are going to read them a short story, but that you are going to stop before it is over. You will want them to draw a picture of what they think will be the next thing to happen in the story. Direct them to keep their pictures secret until it is time to share with the class.

Distribute paper and crayons; then tell the following story:

"Jess and Nan were playing with the ball on the playground. Jess accidentally kicked Nan in the leg, but she thought that he meant to hurt her. Nan hit Jess and started to yell at him . . . ."

From *Games Children Should Play*, © 1980, Mary K. Cihak and Barbara J. Heron, and Goodyear Publishing Co., Inc.

Conduct a short discussion, eliciting from students the likely consequences of Nan's hitting. Ask them to think about how Nan and Jess were feeling. Direct them to draw what happened next.

When students have completed their drawings, allow them to share their pictures, telling what they think happened next and how each character felt. After the sharing, summarize the discussion by pointing out that hitting and fighting almost always hurt people and hurt their feelings and friendships. Suggest that there are better ways to solve problems. Tell them that in the next lesson they will be discovering new ways to solve problems.

Save the pictures for the following lesson.

LANGUAGE ARTS / SOCIAL STUDIES / SEEING CONSEQUENCES / ART

WHAT WILL HAPPEN THEN?—PART II
(Level I)

Goal:

To understand that there are positive consequences to "talking out" problems.

Background:

Many times youngsters seem to know only one way to deal with problem situations. They are in fact often surprised to learn that there are many ways people can deal with the same situation and that people can choose how they will behave. By understanding that there are many different ways that they can behave and by practicing some of these options through role playing, youngsters can increase their repertoire of possible appropriate behavior.

Materials:

Student drawings from "What Will Happen Then?—Part I"; drawing paper and crayons for each student.

Procedure:

Review the "What Will Happen Then?—Part I" story and the consequences as predicted by the children. Remind students that they have learned how using hitting to solve problems usually results in further unhappiness.

Read the story again:

"Jess and Nan were playing ball on the playground. Jess accidentally kicked Nan in the leg, but she thought that he meant to hurt her . . ."

Ask the students if they can think of ways that Nan and Jess could solve their problem so that they could each feel happier. (Possible solutions include: Nan could tell Jess how she feels; Jess could apologize; Nan could ask why he did that; Jess could ask Nan if she is hurt, because he didn't mean to hurt her; Jess could offer to take Nan to the nurse if she is badly hurt.)

When several suggestions have been made, select three or four ideas to be role played. Ask students to role play the selected solutions. After each demonstration, ask the class if the solution would solve the problem. How would each participant feel?

Follow-up:

Direct the students to draw a picture that shows how Jess and Nan feel when they are able to "talk out" their problems. Post both sets of pictures under the titles: "Hitting Makes People Unhappy" and "People Can Feel Happier When They Talk about Their Problems."

LANGUAGE ARTS / SOCIAL STUDIES

GUESS WHAT HAPPENS THEN
(Level II)

Goal:

To become aware of a degree of responsibility people have for what happens to them.

Background:

Similar to the lesson on "I" messages, this and the following activity require consistent, day-by-day reinforcement. Students are taught to analyze a problem by considering their own role in the situation. They are lead to see how what they do may encourage the behavior of others.

Assist students in transferring the lesson to everyday problems. Use the same format to analyze playground, school, and classroom conflicts. Focus attention on the "victim" of the problem: what can he/she do to change the situation?

Materials:

Worksheets (following) for each student (readability level: 2.2, *Spache Readability Formula*).

Procedure:

Present the lesson by asking students if they have ever wondered why people act in certain ways.

Explain that this lesson may help them to find ways they can change a situation. In this lesson, students may learn how to get along better with brothers and sisters, with adults, and with other students.

From *Games Children Should Play*,   © 1980, Mary K. Cihak and Barbara J. Heron, and Goodyear Publishing Co., Inc.

Together, do Story #1, focusing students' attention upon the fact that people usually repeat actions when they receive a response they like.

Divide into groups of four to five students, including able readers in each group, to complete worksheets.

When most groups have completed the task, discuss. Use the technique described in the Related Activity in "A Token–A Turn," Chapter 5.

In discussing the groups' analyses, stress that human behavior is generally predictable, and that we can usually "guess what happens" next. If students persist in offering very unlikely consequences, accept the fact that their consequence *might* indeed happen, but elicit from the group again what *generally* would occur.

Related Activity:

IALAC Filmstrip, Argus Publications.

GUESS WHAT HAPPENS THEN
WORKSHEET

Story 1:

A man walks down the street, saying "Good Morning" to everyone he sees.

If most people smile back and say "Good morning" to him, will the

man say "Good Morning" the next day? _____ Why or why not? ___

_____

If no one answers him, but people frown and walk past him, will

the man say "Good morning" the next day? _____ Why or why not?

_____

_____

Story 2:

A new student is sitting alone in the library. Two of his classmates want to be friendly. They come to share a table with him.

If he turns his head away and pretends not see them, will they try

to be friendly the next day? _____ Why or why not?

_____

If he gets up and moves to the next table, will they try to be friendly

the next day? _____ Why or why not ? _____

_____

If he smiles and quietly says "Hello," will they try to be friendly

the next day? _____ Why or why not? _____

_____

Story 3:

A group teases a classmate about his freckles.

If he cries, will they tease him the next day? _____Why or why

not? _____

If he turns away and walks off, will they tease him the next day?

Why or why not? _____

_____

If he laughs and makes up a story about how he was dropped in the mud as a baby, will they tease him the next day? _____Why or why not? _____

If he gets mad and yells at them, will they tease him the next day?

_____Why or why not? _____

_____

Story 4:

Brad comes home early from softball practice. His older sister is fixing dinner. He begins to set the table.

If she says, "Well, it's about time you helped around here," will he

help her another time? _____Why or why not? _____

_____

If she says, "Thanks—I really appreciate your help," will he help

another day? _____Why or why not? _____

_____

If she ignores him, will he help her another day? _____Why or

why not? _____

_____

Story 5:

One of Esperanza's friends frequently pulls her hair. Esperanza doesn't like that, but her friend keeps doing it.

If Esperanza gets very angry and tells her teacher, what will her

friend do? _____

Games Children Should Play

From *Games Children Should Play*, © 1980, Mary K. Cihak and Barbara J. Heron, and Goodyear Publishing Co., Inc.

Why? _____

    If Esperanza says in a whiny voice, "Please don't do that anymore,"

what will her friend do? _____

Why? _____

    If, whenever her friend pulls her hair, Esperanza talks about some-

thing else, what will her friend do? _____

Why? _____

    If, every time it happens, Esperanza walks away, what will her

friend do? _____

Why? _____

    If Esperanza tells her friend she likes her but she doesn't want her
to pull her hair anymore, what will her friend do?

_____

Why? _____

From *Games Children Should Play*, © 1980, Mary K. Cihak and Barbara J. Heron, and Goodyear Publishing Co., Inc.

WHAT ELSE CAN THEY DO?
(Level II)

Goal:

To learn ways to change situations by changing the "victim's" response.

Materials:

Worksheet for each student (following; readability level: 2.1, *Spache Readability Formula*; flashlight.)

Procedure:

Review the previous lesson, stressing that people usually repeat actions when they receive a response they like.

Explain that sometimes it is hard to understand why people like a certain response. Pose an example: "A four-year-old child teases his older brother. Each time, his older brother yells loudly at him. Why might the younger brother like that response?"

If possible, elicit from the students the likelihood that the young child is looking for his older brother's attention.

Discuss the human need for attention, respect, recognition.

Ask: "What happens if people feel ignored, or not worthwhile, or not respected?" Point out, if necessary, that if people don't get attention for doing the right thing, they may seek attention in annoying ways.

Distribute the worksheet, "What Else Can They Do?" Recall that in solving problems, one considers what each person in the problem wants or needs.

Students complete the worksheets individually or in pairs.

When most have finished, prepare to discuss the worksheet by reviewing the Listening Skills, described in "Spotlight," Chapter 3. Choose an observer to shine the flashlight on each speaker as a reminder of the need to focus attention on the contributor. Discuss the worksheet, concentrating on ways in which the "victim" could change each situation. Help sudents to see the importance of paying attention to appropriate or pleasing behavior. Example: In problem #1, Kris may:

1. Work harder to give her sister attention during other times of the day;

2. Not yell at her when she interrupts, but quietly ask her to leave the room;

3. Praise her when she does not interrupt—take her for a walk, give her a treat, etc.;

4. Tell her sister in advance that she is going to be on the phone. Tell her that if she doesn't disturb Kris while she is on the phone, Kris will play a game of cards with her afterwards.

From *Games Children Should Play*, © 1980, Mary K. Cihak and Barbara J. Heron, and Goodyear Publishing Co., Inc.

WHAT ELSE CAN THEY DO?
WORKSHEET

Problem 1:

Kris's four-year-old sister bothers her every time she talks on the phone with her friends. Kris yells at her, but she does it again and again.

What might Kris's sister want? _____

What else can Kris do about her sister's behavior? _____

_____

_____

Problem 2:

Bruce's eight-year-old brother argues with him about almost everything. If Bruce looks out the window and says, "It's going to rain," his brother says, "Oh, no, it's not!" Bruce argues every time, but his brother keeps disagreeing.

What might Bruce's brother want? _____

What else can Bruce do? _____

_____

Problem 3:

A group of her classmates tease Ana because she is taller than the others in her class. Every time they tease her, Ana teases them back about something.

What might Ana's classmates want? _____

What else can Ana do? _____

_____

Problem 4:

Jim and Bill have been friends for five years. They get along well unless Jim plays softball at recess with other classmates. Then Bill interrupts, heckling Jim from the sidelines. He shouts, "You're going to miss again." Every time, Jim gets angry, yells at Bill, and leaves the game upset.

What might Bill want? _____

What else can Jim do? _____

_____

From *Games Children Should Play*, © 1980, Mary K. Cihak and Barbara J. Heron, and Goodyear Publishing Co., Inc

WHAT COULD YOU DO?
(Level I)

Goal:

To see a variety of ways to solve problems.

Procedure:

This lesson is intended to be used over several class periods, using one or two role plays a day.

Review the lesson on brainstorming. Tell the students that because they are now able to name several ways to behave in a situation, they are ready to practice ways to solve other problems as well.

Read one of the following problems aloud. Ask the students what they could do in such a situation. (You may wish to write the suggestions on the chalkboard.) Then select three of the students' solutions for role plays. At the end of each role play ask: "What might happen next?" and "How would each person feel?"

SUGGESTED ROLE PLAYS:

1. What ways can you use to decide who will be first player in a game?
2. Your friend has loaned you something and you have lost it. What can you do?
3. What can you play with someone who is in a wheelchair?
4. What can you play with someone who cannot see?
5. What can you play with someone who cannot hear?
6. Your friend told you that he/she would play with you, but now he/she is playing with someone else. What can you do?

In subsequent sessions, derive ideas from actual classroom or playground problems.

WHAT ELSE CAN YOU DO?
(Level II)

Goal:

To learn ways to change a personal situation by changing one's own response.

Materials:

One 4 × 6 card for each student.

Procedure:

Review the previous lesson, stressing the power people have to change situations.

Ask students to think of a problem they have which they wish to change. Explain that they will work in groups to solve the problems, and that they will not put their names on their problems.

Give each student an index card. Tell them to divide the card into two columns, heading the columns thus:

WHAT THE OTHER PERSON DOES   WHAT I DO THEN

In the first column, the students are to write what the other person (no name) involved in their problem does that they do not like. In the second column, they are to write what they do about it. Refer to the previous worksheet for examples as necessary.

Form groups of six to eight. Designate a leader for each group. Students place their index cards face down in the center of the group, then shuffle them.

As in "Sharing the Conversation," Chapter 3, provide each small group with a tennis ball which represents the right to speak.

One at a time, the group leader picks up a card and reads it. He/she asks the group to suggest other things the writer of the card might do to change the situation.

Discuss likely consequences to the proposed solutions. Encourage students to evaluate situations by asking the questions: Is this solution respectful of oneself? Is this solution respectful of others?

Follow-up:

Direct students to write in the journals: "The solution my group gave that I plan to try is ———————————————————————."

Establish a "Dear Abby" bulletin board. Students post their problem situations, and others offer suggestions for change.

A CELEBRATION: "I'M PROUD"
(Level I)

Goal:

To develop self-confidence.

Materials:

Copies of the following worksheets for each child; bulletin board. (Optional, photograph of each child.)

Procedure:

Discuss with the students what they have learned this year about communication and other skills. Encourage them to think about some things they do well. Assure them that they should feel proud of these accomplishments and skills.

Direct the students to illustrate with sketches or drawings accomplishments which they are proud of at school and at home.

When the students have finished, post their drawings on the bulletin board. If you have a photograph of each child, "I'm Proud" sketches can be posted under the photographs.

I'M PROUD

I can do these things at school.

I'M PROUD

I can do these things at home.

A CELEBRATION: "I'M PROUD"
(Level II)

Goal:

To build self-confidence.

Procedure:

Ask students to write in their journals things of which they can be proud. Or, direct the students to complete the following sentences:

I'm proud of these things I've done for my friends:

I'm proud of these things I've done for my parents:

I'm proud of these things I've done in school:

I'm proud of these things I've done for ecology:

Volunteers may post all or part of their lists on a class bulletin board. Illustrations may accompany the pride lines.

FEEDBACK FORM FOR CHAPTER 6

When I try to solve problems, I think I need to _____

_____

_____.

I feel I _____

because I _____.

_____
(Name)

FEEDBACK FORM FOR CLASS DISCUSSIONS

In class discussion, I'm best at _____

_____.

I need to improve _____

_____.

I contributed to my discussion group by _____

_____

_____.

One idea that I thought was important in our discussion was _____

_____

_____.

_____
(Name)

7 Becoming Assertive

Before beginning the lessons in this chapter, Level I and II students should be able to:

Identify and label primary feelings they are experiencing;

Use the pronoun "I" to express responsibility for feelings and ideas;

Look directly at the person to whom they speak;

Participate as listening, alert members of an audience during role plays or demonstrations.

In addition, students at Level II should be able to:

Use the brainstorming technique to discover possible solutions to a problem;

Predict probable consequences to particular actions or choices.

This point in the communications training program is a good time to consider the needs of individual students and of the class as a whole. The table which follows, "Trouble Shooting," lists possible problems in group discussions and particular lessons or techniques which, when repeated now, may help to remedy each problem.

This chapter directly teaches elements of courtesy and appropriate timing before it introduces practice in asserting oneself. Thus, the background of mutually respectful communication is set. As in the problem-solving chapter, the use of role plays allows students practice in assertiveness and provides them with immediate feedback or evaluation of their attempts.

These lessons are written with the conviction that most students' apparent lack of courtesy or respect is actually a lack of skills training. When discourtesy is viewed as clumsiness or ineptness, it can be remedied. Assertiveness training attempts to give children a middle ground between being aggressive and being passive. As diverse as their needs may appear, each of the following students demonstrates a need to be taught clear and honest communication of his/her feelings and needs:

160

The student who habitually runs to the teacher or another adult to report conflicts with peers and is unable to resolve conflicts personally, relying instead upon the adult "judge" and "courtroom."

The student who tends to be explosive in dealing with anger, who is unable to express frustration while the situation is still only slightly provoking and whose resentment builds and builds.

The student who is easily manipulated by peers or by one friend and who appears usually unable to identify his/her own ideas or feelings.

The student who frequently falls into the role of the "victim" and projects a sense of helplessness.

The student who appears demanding, interrupting often to ask for assistance.

The student who is passive and quiet, who rarely initiates a conversation.

The student who hurts the feelings of others in standing up for his/her own rights.

While several lessons in this chapter have been indicated as appropriate for Level I students, the majority of the assertiveness training lessons are intended to meet the needs of Level II students. Teachers of younger or less mature students may informally teach skills that promote direct and honest communication. One particular way of informal teaching is by supplying children with appropriate words for expressing their feelings. The following example shows how the teacher might intervene in daily playground or classroom disputes to model and support assertive communication among even very young children:

OPTION ONE:
Teacher supplies exact words and monitors the resulting dialogue.

> **Student:**
> "Alicia's calling me names."
>
> **Teacher:**
> "Look at her and say to her, 'I don't like it when you call me names.' "
>
> **Student:**
> (to Alicia) "I don't like it when you call me names."
>
> **Teacher:**
> "Say to her, 'I feel hurt when you do that.' "
>
> **Student:**
> (to Alicia) "I feel hurt when you do that."

OPTION TWO:
A progressively more difficult learning; teacher provides direction, but not the exact words to be used.

From *Games Children Should Play*,   © 1980, Mary K. Cihak and Barbara J. Heron, and Goodyear Publishing Co., Inc.

Student:

"Alicia's calling me names."

Teacher:

"Look at her and tell her you don't like it when she calls you names."

Student:

(to Alicia) "I don't like it when you call me names."

Teacher:

"Now tell her how you feel about it."

Student:

(to Alicia) "I feel sad when you do that."

OPTION THREE:

Still more difficult than the preceding; teacher merely provides direction.

Student:

"Alicia's calling me names."

Teacher:

"You need to tell Alicia what you don't like and how you feel about her doing that."

At Levels I and II, each lesson is considered essential to the continuity of the chapter. Maintain reasonable expectations for student performance in the practice role plays. As adults most of us continue to communicate assertively in our own lives. It is inappropriate to expect children to perform perfectly. Instead, reinforce with positive attention even the smallest steps toward assertion. Call attention to the children's effective posture, eye contact, and "I" statements. Reinforce their attempts to respect the rights of others as well as their own rights. Understand that a certain amount of clumsiness or awkwardness is present in any new learning, and the learning of communication skills is no exception.

You may extend the learning from formal lessons by calling attention to assertiveness you observe in children's interactions. "John, I noticed that you told Sam just how you felt and what you needed," is a powerful recognition of the child's growth.

TROUBLE SHOOTING

Before beginning the assertiveness training, take time to diagnose weaknesses in students' communication skills. Use the table on the next page to locate lessons that can be repeated now and throughout the assertiveness unit to reinforce weak areas.

WHAT'S WRONG	TRY RECYCLING:
Students have difficulty expressing feelings clearly.	(Level I) My Own Book, p. 18 (Level II) The Journal, p. 21 (Level I) ABC of Feelings, p. 22 (Level I) Say "I" Circle, p. 114 (Level II) Messages, Scripts, p. 117
Students do not listen to each other, in class meetings or in small groups.	Nonverbal Signs of Listening, p. 62 What Gets in the Way of Communication—Part II follow-up, p. 46 (Level I) Sharing Feelings, p. 50 (Level II) Listening Triads procedure, or Related Activity, p. 51 (Level II) Class Meetings and Observers, p. 52 Spotlight, p. 53 Sharing the Conversation, p. 58 A Token—A Turn, Related Activity to reinforce specific elements of listening, p. 113
Students do not relate to one another's contributions; they direct comments to the teacher instead.	(Level II) Class Meetings and Observers, procedure, instructional segment, p. 52 Spotlight, p. 53 Sharing the Conversation, p. 58 Back-to-Back Puzzles, Related Activity, p. 108 (Level II) Discussion Game, p. 112
No one talks, or a few students monopolize the conversation.	Sharing the Conversation, p. 58 Let's Tell a Story, p. 59 A Token—A Turn, p. 113
During role plays, the audience is not observant.	Mirror Images, p. 64 Watch and Join Me, p. 77 Tone of Voice Guessing Game, p. 94 See introduction, Chapter 6.
During problem solving, a few students offer unrealistic or purely humorous solutions.	(Level II) Seeing Consequences, p. 137
Students' expressions of feelings take the form of accusations.	(Level I) Say "I" Circle, p. 114 (Level II) Say "I", pp. 116

LANGUAGE ARTS

COURTESY
(Levels I and II)

Goal:

To recognize the importance of courtesy in communication.

Materials:

Script, following.

Procedure:

Discuss with the students the importance that courtesy plays in the way people respond to each other. Remind students that it is not only what is said or when it is said, but *how* it is said that gets the message across. Courtesy includes voice tone and use of polite words. Demonstrate for the students the importance of courteous words by speaking the following phrases (use a similar, even tone of voice for each phrase). Ask: Which phrase sounded more courteous or respectful?

Give me that.
May I please have that?

No.
No, thank you.

What do ya want?
Can I help you with something?

Who's this?
Who's calling, please?

Move your foot in!
Would you please move your foot out of the aisle so I can pass?

Demonstrate the importance of voice tone with the following phases. (Say each sentence twice. First, use a sarcastic or hostile tone of voice; the second time use a pleasant tone.) Ask: Which tone sounded courteous?

Excuse me!

What did you say?

I want to go to the movie tonight.

I'd like to talk with you.

I'd like that.

After each section of the following script is read, direct students to predict what responses could be expected from the situation. Ask:

What does each person feel?

What does each want?

What might happen next? Why?

After the scripts have been read and discussed, ask for volunteers to show how they would deal with courtesy in the following situations. Point out respectful words and tone.

You'd like to have a second helping of peaches for lunch.

You'd like to use the teacher's large scissors.

You'd like to have fried chicken for dinner.

A friend has asked you to come over to his house. You can't come.

When the art paper was being distributed, you were skipped.

From *Games Children Should Play,* © 1980, Mary K. Cihak and Barbara J. Heron, and Goodyear Publishing Co., Inc.

COURTESY SCRIPTS

1(a)

SCENE:
Bruce's dad has been working late every night this week. He comes into the house at 9:00.

Bruce:
(angry tone of voice) Why don't you ever take me fishing? Everybody else gets to go fishing!

1(b)

Bruce:
Dad, are you too tired to talk for a little while? Or could I ask you something at breakfast tomorrow?

Dad:
No, it's OK. What is it you wanted to know, Bruce?

Bruce:
Well, the kids say the fishing in the lake has been really good this **week.** Do you think we could go fishing together this weekend?

2(a)

SCENE:
Classroom. Howard is going to sharpen his pencil. Lisa's chair is in the aisle, and he can't get by.

Howard:
(angry tone of voice) Move your chair!

2(b)

Howard:
(courteous tone of voice) Excuse me, Lisa, could you please move your chair? I can't pass.

166

Games Children Should Play

SCENE:
Recess. Students are just leaving the class.

Student:
(indignant tone of voice) Mrs. Brown, you marked my paper wrong when my answer was right. I deserve a better grade.

3(b)

Student:
(courteous tone of voice) Excuse me, Mrs. Brown, is this a good time to talk to you?

Mrs. Brown:
Surely. I have a few minutes right now. What can I do for you?

Student:
I was checking over my spelling paper that I got back this morning. I double-checked this word, and I can't find anything wrong with it. I think you made a mistake when you marked it wrong. Would you look at it?

Mrs. Brown:
Hmm, let me see. Why, I must have been going too fast. You're right; this is correct.

Student:
Would you raise my grade then, please?

COURTEOUS WORDS—MOBILES
(Levels I and II)

Goals:

To learn the importance of expressing respect for other people by using courteous words. To make a visual reminder to use courteous words.

Materials:

Poster board; paper plates; yarn; dowels, if available; scissors; black pens.

Procedure:

Review with the students the importance of using courteous words. Elicit from them a list of common courteous words. List those on the board. Direct the students to work in small groups. Plan which courtesy word they will choose to remind people to use. Then design a face or person using that word. Show the examples on the following page. When the students have planned their hanging pictures, provide them with paper plates and yarn for making the faces and poster board for the body and the words.

When the mobiles are completed, hang them around the room as visual reminders to use courteous words.

Related Reading:

Sesyle Joslin, *What Do You Say, Dear?* (New York: Young Scott Books, 1958).

(two plates stapled together, with the words coming from between them.)

TIMING
(Levels I and II)

Goal:

To recognize the importance of timing in communication.

Materials:

Scripts (following).

Procedure:

Discuss with the students the importance that timing plays in the way people respond to each other. Ask them to imagine how they would respond to you if you wanted one of them to run an errand at the same time he/she was supposed to be working in the cafeteria (or the office or safety patrol). How would the student's response be different if you asked for help when that student had some free time? Ask them to imagine how you might respond if you were talking with a parent and one of them interrupted to ask for help with yesterday's math lesson. How might you respond if the student asked you for help when you weren't busy or talking to anyone?

Direct the class to listen to each section of the following scripts and predict the responses that can be expected in each situation. What does each person feel? What does each want? What might happen next? Why?

After the scripts have been read and discussed, ask for volunteers to show how to deal with timing in the following situations:

You need to talk to the principal. Her door is open, but she is busy writing.

You want your mother to write you an absence excuse because you were sick yesterday. Your mother is talking on the telephone.

You want your friend to come over to your house this afternoon. He is in the middle of a soccer game.

You want your little sister to go next door on an errand for you. You are in a hurry. Your sister is playing with one of her friends.

You are supposed to pick up homework for a friend who is sick. Every time you think about it, your teacher seems very busy.

From *Games Children Should Play,* © 1980, Mary K. Cihak and Barbara J. Heron, and Goodyear Publishing Co., Inc.

TIMING SCRIPTS
(Level I)

1(a)

SCENE:
Home. The baby is crying and the food is burning on the stove. Mother is taking care of the food.

Child:
Mommy, Mommy, can I go over to Casey's next Saturday and go swimming?

1(b)

SCENE:
Home. The family is sitting around the table eating dinner.

Child:
Mommy, may I go over to Casey's house next Saturday and go swimming?

2(a)

SCENE:
Home. Mother and Dad are getting ready to have company. They are hurrying to get ready before their guests arrive. The telephone is ringing.

Randy:
Dad, can you help me fix my wagon now?

2(b)

SCENE:
Dad and Randy are riding in the car together.

Randy:
Dad, when can you fix my wagon? Is it possible for you to do it today?

3(a)

SCENE:
Mother is talking on the telephone.

Holly:
Mom! Mom! Guess what happened at school today! I got to be in a puppet show!

From *Games Children Should Play,*   © 1980, Mary K. Cihak and Barbara J. Heron, and Goodyear Publishing Co., Inc.

SCENE:
Mother is talking on the telephone. Holly waits until she hangs up.

> **Holly:**
> Mom, guess what happened at school today! I got to be in a puppet show! Everybody liked it.

4(a)

SCENE:
On the playground. A student has been hurt and is crying. The teacher is helping him get a bandage. Janet comes to the scene.

> **Janet:**
> Teacher (tugs on the teacher's sleeve), Teacher! Mr. Sun! When may I move my desk so that I may sit by Annie?

4(b)

SCENE:
On the playground. The teacher is standing watching the students play.

> **Janet:**
> Mr. Sun, when may I move my desk so that I may sit by Annie?

5(a)

SCENE:
Classroom. The students are working. The teacher is talking with a parent. Rodney walks up to them.

> **Rodney:**
> Mrs. Johnson, when are we going to have a class party?

5(b)

SCENE:
Classroom. At the end of sharing time, Rodney raises his hand.

> **Rodney:**
> Mrs. Johnson, when are we going to have a class party?

From *Games Children Should Play,* © 1980, Mary K. Cihak and Barbara J. Heron, and Goodyear Publishing Co., Inc.

TIMING SCRIPTS
(Level II)

1(a)

SCENE:
Mr. Santos has just given a lesson about fractions. The worksheets on
that lesson are now being distributed to the students.

Mr. Santos:
Please raise your hand if you need any help with the page of fractions.
I'll get to each of you as quickly as I can.

Student:
(pleasant tone of voice) Mr. Santos, I checked this spelling word that you
marked wrong last week on my spelling test, and it is spelled correctly.
Would you please look at it and change my grade?

1(b)

Mr. Santos:
Please raise your hand if you need any help with the page of fractions.
I'll get around to each of you as quickly as I can.

Student:
Mr. Santos, could I talk with you a few minutes sometime later today?
I need to see you about my spelling test.

2(a)

SCENE:
In the kitchen at Annette's house. Annette's mother is expecting company
for dinner at 6:00. It's 5:30 and she is hurrying to get ready.

Mother:
Annette, please set the table for dinner. Our company will be here soon.

Annette:
Mother, may I spend the night Friday at Louise's? And then may I have
some money to go shopping Saturday?

2(b)

Mother:
Annette, please set the table for dinner. Our guests will be here soon.

Annette:
I know you're busy, but do you have a minute to talk about this weekend?
Or shall I wait until after dinner to ask you something?

SCENE:
Mr. O'Gill is teaching a reading lesson to a group of students. They are
talking about the story they just read.

> **Mr. O'Gill:**
> If you were Jane in this story, what might you do differently from the
> way Jane did it in the story?

> **Student:**
> Mr. O'Gill, may I change desks? I want to sit by my friend, Don.

3(b)

SCENE:
Mr. O'Gill is excusing the class for recess. Most of the students are leaving
the room.

> **Student:**
> Mr. O'Gill, could I talk with you a minute?

> **Mr. O'Gill:**
> Yes, this is a good time. What can I do for you?

> **Student:**
> I would like to change desks so that I may sit with Don. May I do that?

4(a)

SCENE:
Dad has just started to take a shower. Lou knocks on the bathroom door.

> **Lou:**
> Dad! Hey Dad! Dad! (Dad turns off the shower.)

> **Dad:**
> What's the matter, Lou?

> **Lou:**
> Dad, do you want me to fix you a cup of coffee?

4(b)

SCENE:
Dad comes from the bathroom after having taken his shower. Lou knocks
on his bedroom door.

> **Lou:**
> Dad, would you like me to fix you a cup of coffee?

From *Games Children Should Play,*   © 1980, Mary K. Cihak and Barbara J. Heron, and Goodyear Publishing Co., Inc.

DEVELOPING AWARENESS OF SOCIAL CONTEXT
(Levels I and II)

Goal:

To develop the understanding that different social situations demand different types of behavior.

Procedure:

Tell the students that our behavior needs to change depending on where we are and who we are with.

Ask the students to observe as you pretend to watch TV when you are home alone. (Act out eating noisily, changing the channels back and forth to watch two shows at a time, walking around singing, talking on the phone, etc.) Discuss: If you had been watching TV with another person, how might he/she have felt if you had behaved that way? What might the other person have needed? How might your behavior need to change if you had been watching TV with another person?

Discuss appropriate behavior for such places as the supermarket, the shopping mall, the movie theater, restaurants, roller rinks, on buses or planes. Contrast behavior for those places with behavior suitable for one's own back yard or the school playground. Discuss why behavior needs to change with different situations.

Ask for volunteers to role play the following situations. After each role play, discuss who was there and what they needed. How did the behavior need to change as the situation changed?

Show how you would behave if you took a message to the school office and the secretary didn't seem busy and nobody else was there. Then show how your behavior would change if there were several people in the office and the secretary was very busy.

Show how you might behave in your own living room. Then show how your behavior would need to change if you were a guest in someone else's living room.

Show how you would behave if you were in a library and there were lots of people reading and studying there. What if you and the librarian were the only people in the library?

Show how you would behave at a football game. Show how your behavior would be different at an orchestra concert. Then show how that would be different from how you would behave at a rock concert.

Show how you might visit with your mother if there were just the two of you. Show how your behavior would be different if your mother had a guest who was visiting her.

From *Games Children Should Play*,   © 1980, Mary K. Cihak and Barbara J. Heron, and Goodyear Publishing Co., Inc.

ART / LANGUAGE ARTS / SOCIAL STUDIES

ANGER IS A FEELING
(Levels I and II)

Goal:

To recognize and accept anger as a legitimate feeling.

Materials:

Drawing paper; pencils; crayons or paint.

Procedure:

Talk with students about anger—when they've felt it, how it feels. Assume that there is nothing wrong with feeling angry. Still, it is an uncomfortable feeling, and sometimes it is hard to handle. Frequently when people have a problem, anger is one of the feelings they have. Anger is a sign that something has gone wrong.

On their papers, students illustrate how anger feels. When their pictures are complete, have them take turns telling people in a small group about their picture.

Explain to the students that by the end of this unit they will have discovered some ways to handle their anger. They will learn how to solve problems when they or someone else feels angry.

**Related Activity
(Level II):**

In journals, complete these sentences:

The last time I was angry was _____.

When I feel angry, I _____.

I often feel angry about _____.

Related Reading:

Alvyn Freed, *T.A. for Tots, T.A. for Kids,* (Sacramento, Calif.: Jalmar Press, Inc., 1973).

LANGUAGE ARTS / SOCIAL STUDIES

EXPRESSING ANGER: DO'S AND DON'TS
(Level II)

Goal:

To learn a structure for expressing anger.

176

Games Children Should Play

Materials:

List of "Do's and Don'ts." Worksheet following; readability level: 2.2, *Spache Readability Formula).*

Background:

You may wish to read *The Intimate Enemy* by George Bach, since it provides full background for "fair fighting."

Procedure:

Introduce the lesson by inviting students to complete the sentences: "One thing that bothers me is _____" and "I feel angry when _____." Emphasize that expressing anger can help solve problems: telling someone how you feel about what he/she did builds communication and gives that person a chance to change. Elicit examples from school and home situations which improved after someone was honest about his/her anger or frustration.

Clarify that situations do not improve just because someone expresses his/her anger. The *way* in which feelings are expressed can make the difference. The key to expressing anger is to do it without hurting the other person. Explain: showing respect for a person when one is angry is difficult and takes practice.

EXPRESSING ANGER—DO'S AND DON'TS

DO respect the other person by:

1. Talking to the person in private.
2. Saying what he/she did that you did not like.
3. Telling how you feel about it.
4. Telling what you want the person to change.

DON'T hurt the other person by:

1. Talking about the past.
2. Using put-downs.
3. Using threats.
4. Telling other people about it.

Tell the students that in the following skit (Script 1, following) you (or another person) are pretending to be a student who is angry because someone called you a name. You will read the script slowly two times. The first time, students are to listen carefully and try to spot how you show lack of respect for the person. During the second reading, students are to raise their hands as soon as they hear you break a rule. (During this second reading, stop after each noted infraction and discuss.)

Repeat the skit process with Script 2.

Distribute copies of the worksheet. Discuss Problem #1 as a group. Students complete the rest of the worksheet individually or in pairs. When finished, discuss the responses together.

Follow-up:

Place the "Do's and Don'ts" list near the pow-wow rug.

From *Games Children Should Play*, © 1980, Mary K. Cihak and Barbara J. Heron, and Goodyear Publishing Co., Inc.

EXPRESSING ANGER: DO'S AND DON'TS SCRIPTS
(Level II)

1

ESTABLISH SCENE:

(Talks in public)

You are a student. David just called you a name, then walked away. You stand up and shout across the room to him:

(Doesn't say
"I feel . . .")
(Talks about the past)
(Uses put-downs)
(Talks about the past)
(Uses threats)

(Doesn't say exactly
what the person can do
to change)

"You make me so mad. I've had enough of your teasing. You're always making fun of me and it's not right. Everyone says you're a bully. You tease Joan and Betty all the time, too. Why, you have been teasing me all my life—well, at least a year. Nobody likes you any more. And furthermore, you borrowed paper and pencils from me last week. You've owed me ten cents since last month. If you don't straighten up fast, I'm going to get all my friends to stop speaking to you."

2

ESTABLISH SCENE:

(Talks in public)

You are walking down the aisle of the classroom when you stumble on Kristi's foot. You stumble a bit and yell out:

(Doesn't say how
he/she feels)
(Talks about the past)
(Uses put-downs)
(Uses threats)

(Doesn't say exactly
what the person can do
to change)

"How dare you trip me on purpose like that? I know that wasn't an accident. You hit innocent people and trip them all the time. I saw you trip Jim just last week, and that was no accident. You are mean and a trouble maker. I'll never be your friend again. There's nobody in this class who'll be your friend again because I'm letting everyone know you do mean things. And I'm getting my older brother to take care of you."

From *Games Children Should Play*,   © 1980, Mary K. Cihak and Barbara J. Heron, and Goodyear Publishing Co., Inc.

EXPRESSING ANGER
WORKSHEET

Problem 1:

Anita is playing basketball with her friends. Betty runs through the game, right in front of Anita. After the bell rings, Anita goes to Betty and says:

I feel _____because you _____

_____

_____,

and I want you to _____

_____.

Problem 2:

The teacher keeps calling Janice by the name of her older sister, Jolene. Janice finds a quiet time to speak to her teacher:

I feel _____because you _____

_____

_____,

and I'd like you to _____

_____.

Problem 3:

Solomon is playing around on the field and not watching what he is doing. He kicks a ball backwards, and it hits Chris on the head. Chris goes over to Solomon and speaks to him alone. He says:

I feel _____because you _____

_____

_____,

and I'd like you to _____

_____.

From *Games Children Should Play*,   © 1980, Mary K. Cihak and Barbara J. Heron, and Goodyear Publishing Co., Inc.

Problem 4:

John was walking across the room when Jim poked him with a pencil. John stops him and says:

I feel _____because you _____

_____

_____,

and I want you to _____

_____.

Problem 5:

Andy keeps taking Juan's cap and wearing it. Juan sees him alone before school one day and says to him:

I feel _____because you _____

_____

_____,

and I want you to _____

_____.

Problem 6:

Sarah has a speech problem. Ken makes fun of her and calls her "stupid." Sarah says to him in private:

I feel _____ because you _____

_____

_____,

and I want you to _____

_____.

From *Games Children Should Play*,   © 1980, Mary K. Cihak and Barbara J. Heron, and Goodyear Publishing Co., Inc.

Problem 7:

Mable is working on a project with Eileen and Karen. Every time Mable suggests something, the others say, "No, no, we're going to do it this way." Mable tells the group that she wants them to stop what they are doing for a few minutes, because she wants to talk to them. She says:

I feel _____ because you _____

_____

_____,

and I'd like you to _____

_____.

Problem 8:

Damon is working on a committee with Chang and Berta. Every time the committee members start to discuss their job, Damon is either drawing or looking out the window. When Chang and Berta start to work, Damon tells them that he doesn't understand what they are doing; then he walks off to sit by himself. Chang goes over to him and says:

I feel _____ because you _____

_____

_____,

and I want you to _____

_____.

From *Games Children Should Play*,   © 1980, Mary K. Cihak and Barbara J. Heron, and Goodyear Publishing Co., Inc.

RECOGNIZING ASSERTIVENESS
(Level II)

Goal:

To recognize assertive behavior.

Materials:

Chalkboard or chart on which alternative behavior styles (see below) are written; two copies of scripts, following.

Background:

In dealing with this and subsequent exercises, you will want to be aware of three basic conflict-resolving styles: passivity, aggression, and assertion. Each of these styles includes typical behavior patterns. In teaching students assertiveness, respect for oneself as well as for others is the significant concept to transmit.

Passive behavior (nonassertion) is characterized by a lack of respect for oneself. The passive person does not express himself or herself honestly. He/she allows others to violate or disregard his/her needs. He/she appears apologetic, using a whiny voice and monotone. His/her posture is often slumped, his/her eyes downcast.

Aggressive behavior is characterized by a lack of respect for others. The aggressive person "puts down" others, disregarding their feelings and their needs. He/she often speaks loudly, avoids "I" messages, blaming others instead, and may fold his/her arms over his/her chest.

Sometimes aggressive people are indirect in their aggression. They have the same disrespect for others although they do not show it openly. They manipulate or trick others in order to get their own way.

Assertive people respect themselves and others. The assertive person is generally confident, calm, clear. He/she can speak of his/her own needs and allows others to do so, also. His/her posture is straight, but not stiff. He/she uses good timing and clear "I" messages.

Procedure:

Discuss the concepts of respect and disrespect with students. Elicit from students that respect does not necessarily mean that one always agrees with another. Respect can be illustrated by the famous quotation from Voltaire, "I disapprove of what you say, but I will defend to the death your right to say it."

Discuss the following three behavior styles with the students, adding as much of the preceding background notes and vocabulary as seems appropriate for the students' ages and levels of comprehension.

PEOPLE WHO DO NOT RESPECT
THEMSELVES (PASSIVE):

Don't meet their own needs;

Seem helpless and "picked on";

Use whiny voices;

Have slumped posture and look down.

*PEOPLE WHO DO NOT RESPECT OTHERS
(AGGRESSIVE):*

Do not respect the needs of others;

Are bullies;

"Put down" others;

Use loud voices;

Are pushy;

Force their wants on others.

*PEOPLE WHO RESPECT THEMSELVES AND
RESPECT OTHERS (ASSERTIVE):*

Express their own needs and attempt to understand the needs of others also;

Are courteous;

Appear confident;

Use good timing;

Use straight body posture and look directly at others;

Use "I" messages;

Try to work things out, or compromise.

When the students understand the basic differences in behavior styles, direct them to consider the situation in the script (following) and its varied solutions.

Students are to categorize Thelma's solutions according to (1) Disrespect of Self, (2) Disrespect of Others, (3) Respect of Self and Respect of Others.

After each segment of the script, ask: "Does Thelma respect herself?" "Does she respect Kim?"

ASSERTIVENESS SCRIPTS
(Level II)

SCENE:
Kim never seems to have a pencil and regularly borrows one from Thelma.
Kim seldom remembers to return the borrowed pencil, or if she does, its
lead is broken and it is much shorter than when she borrowed it.

1

(Disrespects others. Aggressive.) (Thelma speaks in a loud voice.)

Kim:
Hey, Thelma, may I borrow a pencil? I lost mine.

Thelma:
No way! You never return pencils and you're inconsiderate. You never
come prepared. You can just sit there while we take the test. You'll get
an F, and I'll be glad.

Kim:
Aw, come on, Thelma. I'll return it, I promise.

Thelma:
Not a chance. You deserve to flunk!

2

(Disrespects self. Passive.) (Thelma speaks in a high, thin voice.)

Kim:
Hey, Thelma, may I borrow a pencil? I lost mine.

Thelma:
Well, I don't know.

Kim:
Aw please, I don't know what happened to mine.

Thelma:
Well, I just have this one long pencil. The other one is short.

Kim:
That's O.K. People can only read my writing when I use a long pencil,
so I need the long one.

Thelma:
Well, I just got that pencil, but I guess it's all right.

Kim:
Oh, thanks a lot, Thelma. I'll give it back to you, probably after this
period, or maybe tomorrow.

184

(Respects self. Respects others. Assertive.) (Thelma speaks in a calm voice.)

Kim:

Hey, Thelma, may I borrow a pencil? I can't find mine.

Thelma:

I don't want to lend you a pencil because when you borrow my pencils, you either forget to return them or the lead is broken.

Kim:

Aw come on, Thelma. We're going to have a test. What am I going to do without a pencil?

Thelma:

I'm sorry, I don't know what you are going to do. I don't want to lend you a pencil because when you borrow my things you don't return them to me in good condition.

Kim:

What if I promise to return it right after the test? Could I borrow one then?

Thelma:

Well, if you really will return the pencil right after the test and if you sharpen it before you return it, you may use my short pencil.

Kim:

Gee, thanks Thelma. I promise. (pause) But you know, the teacher can only read my writing when I use a long pencil.

Thelma:

Well, I'm sorry, Kim, but the short one is the only one that I have that you may use.

From *Games Children Should Play,*   © 1980, Mary K. Cihak and Barbara J. Heron, and Goodyear Publishing Co., Inc.

POSITIVE IMAGING
(Levels I and II)

Goal:

To visualize and practice self-assertion.

Background:

Imagination is a powerful source for helping people to learn new behavior. It is difficult to change behavior and students will be more successful starting at a no-risk level (imaging) and going to a low-risk task (role playing) before they try to do something at a high-risk level (a real life confrontation).

Procedure:

Tell the students that you are going to guide them through some imaginary situations. Ask them to close their eyes and imagine the situation you give them. When they have completed the imaging, they are to open their eyes. You will then ask for a volunteer or two to show the group what he/she did in the situation. (The demonstrating students do a monologue.) If needed, do the first example yourself.

SITUATIONS:

You are on the school bus. Someone you've never seen before sits next to you. Imagine yourself starting a conversation.

You see a group of kids talking together by a swimming pool. Imagine yourself joining their conversation.

You've been to the grocery store. You get about halfway home when you find that you were given the wrong change. Imagine yourself going back and asking for the right change.

The teacher blames you for throwing a paper across the room. You didn't do it. Imagine yourself explaining what happened and telling him/her that you didn't do it.

Your team is up to bat, and a team member hits a home run and brings in two other runs, also. Imagine yourself congratulating your teammate.

Your friend takes a ball from the school. Imagine yourself telling your friend that he/she is to return it.

You are lost in a new town. Imagine yourself asking someone for help.

From *Games Children Should Play*,   © 1980, Mary K. Cihak and Barbara J. Heron, and Goodyear Publishing Co., Inc.

ASSERTIVENESS AT SCHOOL
(Level I)

Goal:

To practice courteous, assertive behavior in representative school situations.

Materials:

Cards (following; readability levels: A, 1.8; B, 3.0; C, 2.4; D, 3.1; E, 2.5; F, 3.2; G, 2.4; H, 3.0; I, 2.7; J, 2.3; K, 2.5; L, 3.0; M, 2.6, *Spache Readability Formula*).

Procedure:

Role playing is most effective in small groups of ten to fifteen students, particularly with youngsters at Level I ages or abilities. If possible, obtain the help of another adult to lead a second group using the following role plays.

Review the importance of timing and courtesy. Ask the students to think about the previous lessons on timing, and how it felt to be interrupted by someone. Mention that there are some situations that are emergencies, when you can't use good timing, such as when you are ill and you might throw-up. In an emergency you can't wait for good timing, and people will understand why you interrupt them.

Tell the students that they are going to act out some situations that might happen at school. Explain that in the plays they will practice good timing and courtesy. Ask another adult or student to help you model the situation described on Card A:

1. Read the directions on the card aloud: "Ask someone to join your game."
2. Demonstrate, with your partner, how to invite someone to play a game with you.

In using Card B, choose one child to play the teacher, Mr. Saito, and one child to play the student, Joe. This time supply the two actors with the words to use. Each actor repeats his line after you.

1. Read Card B aloud: "Tell the teacher that you were absent yesterday, and you want to know what work you should do."
2. Explain to the class that this role play takes place at recess time. Joe, the student, waits until the other students have left the classroom and Mr. Saito doesn't look busy.
3. You turn to Joe: "Joe, you say to Mr. Saito, 'Excuse me, Mr. Saito, is this a good time to talk to you?'" (Joe repeats)

From *Games Children Should Play*,   © 1980, Mary K. Cihak and Barbara J. Heron, and Goodyear Publishing Co., Inc.

4. You turn to Mr. Saito: "Mr. Saito, you can tell Joe this is a good time." (Mr. Saito tells Joe) "Ask Joe what he wants." (Mr. Saito asks)

5. You turn to Joe: "Joe, you say to Mr. Saito, 'I was absent yesterday. Is there some work I should do to catch up? I will take it home tonight to do it.'"

Discuss how timing and courtesy were shown in the role play.

Ask for volunteers to work as partners for the next role plays. It is effective to give more than one group the same situation to demonstrate. Besides increasing the practice that students get, they also observe that there is more than one effective way to assert oneself. Allow about three minutes for practice before summoning them back to the meeting place to give their demonstrations. If a pair isn't able to do the demonstration successfully, return to the procedure used for Cards A and B: either model for them, or supply them with appropriate words to use.

(Note: In this, and in the lessons which follow, reinforce with praise students' efforts towards becoming more assertive. Point out elements of assertiveness in their role plays: confident posture, eye contact, saying "I feel _____" and "I want _____." Communicating assertively can be difficult—encourage even the smallest steps in that direction.)

Ask someone to play in your game.

Assertiveness at School (Level I)

A

Tell the teacher that you were absent yesterday. You want to know what work you should do.

Assertiveness at School (Level I)

B

Games Children Should Play

From *Games Children Should Play*, © 1980, Mary K. Cihak and Barbara J. Heron, and Goodyear Publishing Co., Inc.

Tell someone he/she made a good play in the game.

C

Find out what rules the children use to play tetherball here.

D

You don't understand a math problem. Ask your teacher for help.

E

You told your friend that there was going to be a movie at school today. You find that you are wrong. Tell your friend that you made a mistake.

F

You can't hear from where you are sitting. Ask your teacher to change your seat.

G

You don't understand the teacher's answer to your question. Tell the teacher that you still don't understand. Ask the teacher to explain again.

H

Tell the teacher that you are feeling sick, and you might throw up.

I

The teacher is teaching a reading group. Tell the teacher that you need to go to the bathroom. Explain that you can't wait any longer.

J

Your teacher and some of the parents gave the class a party. Thank one of them.

Assertiveness at School (Level I)

K

The adult on the playground at recess taught you and your friends a new game. Thank him/her for helping you.

Assertiveness at School (Level I)

L

You cannot hear the teacher because your friend is talking to you. Ask your friend not to talk now.

Assertiveness at School (Level I)

M

ASSERTIVENESS AT SCHOOL
(Level II)

Goal:

To practice courteous, assertive behavior in representative school situations.

Materials:

Cards (following; readability levels: A, 2.5; B, 2.7; C, 2.5; D, 2.5; E, 2.8; F, 2.4; G, 2.4; H, 1.9; I, 2.6; J, 2.6; K, 2.0; *Spache Readability Formula*).

Procedures:

Review the process of problem solving.

Remind students that after they have examined the possible consequences of an action and have chosen an appropriate solution, it is time to act. Explain that sometimes, even when people know what they should do or say, they find it difficult to do or say it in a manner that respects their own and others' rights. Practicing with each other helps everyone to see how a variety of solutions might work.

Remind students of the nonverbal and verbal ways of getting the message across: standing or sitting tall, looking directly at a person, using a courteous tone of voice, speaking clearly and confidently, using "I" messages, using considerate timing.

Direct the students to form small groups. Give each group a task card and direct them to role play a desirable solution. Ask:

"How do you think that solution would work?"

"How would *you* have responded if _____had said that to you?"

"Can you think of any other ways this might have been worked out satisfactorily?"

(Note: If a group models an aggressive or passive solution, ask them to try again, or ask someone else to model an assertive response before they try it again.)

For every role play, the test of assertiveness is: Did the actor respect his/her own rights and the rights of others?

(Note: Communicating assertively can be difficult—encourage even the smallest steps in that direction.)

You like the woman who is on yard duty, but your best friends don't like her. They are angry at her because she punished them when they broke the school rules. They are saying mean and untrue things about her. What will you say to them?

A

You really like school, but some of your friends don't. On your way to school one morning, they tell you they're going to skip school and they ask you to come along. What will you say to them?

B

You like to play softball. You go out to the field every recess. You're usually chosen last and that hurts your feelings, but you go ahead and play your best. You are often last to bat, so sometimes you don't get your turn. Tell one of your classmates how you feel and what you want.

C

You feel you have been treated unfairly by the playground supervisor, who benched you for breaking a school rule. You don't feel that the supervisor understood the whole situation. What can you say to her/him?

D

During games at recess, the whole team yells at you when you goof. Other team members aren't perfect, but they don't seem to get yelled at as much as you do. Tell a teammate how you feel and what you want.

E

You especially enjoyed the science lesson that was taught today. Tell the teacher how much you liked it.

F

You are saying goodby to a classroom aide who has been helpful to you and whom you liked very much. Tell that aide how you feel toward him/her and how much you appreciate him/her.

G

Your friend has taken a school baseball home. What will you say to him/her?

H

The teacher wants you to work on a group project. You want to work on the project, but you don't want to work with the group to which you were assigned. Explain this to the teacher.

Assertiveness at School (Level II)   I

Your friends want you to smoke with them. You don't like smoking and you don't want to start that habit, but you like your friends and you want to be with them. Tell them what you are thinking.

Assertiveness at School (Level II)   J

LANGUAGE ARTS / SOCIAL STUDIES

ASSERTIVENESS AT HOME
(Level I)

Goal:

To practice courteous, assertive behavior in representative home situations.

Materials:

Cards (following; readability levels: A, 2.4; B, 2.5; C, 2.1; D, 2.1; E, 2.4; F, 3.1; G, 2.9; H, 2.3; I, 2.5; J, 2.0; K, 2.4; L, 3.0; M, 3.2; N, 2.8; *Spache Readability Formula*).

Procedure:

Elicit from the students the nonverbal and verbal signs of getting the message across confidently and courteously: standing tall, looking directly at the person, remembering courteous timing, using a courteous tone of voice, speaking clearly, using "I . . . ." Stress that assertiveness involves respecting oneself and respecting others.

From *Games Children Should Play*,   © 1980, Mary K. Cihak and Barbara J. Heron, and Goodyear Publishing Co., Inc.

If possible, ask another adult to help you so that your groups may be between ten and fifteen children. Use the same series of role-play procedures described in "Assertiveness at School" Level I:

1. Model a role for the students;
2. Supply the words while students act the roles;
3. Provide free trials for the students.

Discuss the role plays. Were they effective in getting the message across? Did the actors use good timing? Were they courteous?

Your mother fixed a good dinner. Tell her that you liked the dinner.

Assertiveness at Home (Level I)   **A**

Your father helped you wash the dishes. Tell your father that you appreciate his helping you.

Assertiveness at Home (Level I)   **B**

Your baby-sitter took time to play some games with you. Thank him/her for playing with you.

Assertiveness at Home (Level I)   **C**

Some new people moved in next door. You see one of the children outside. Introduce yourself.

Assertiveness at Home (Level I)

D

Your mother has a friend visiting. Your mother left the room for a minute. You come in. Introduce yourself to your mother's friend.

Assertiveness at Home (Level I)

E

Your father lets you have some friends visit your house for a party. He fixes the food for your friends and makes them feel welcome. After your friends have gone, thank your father.

Assertiveness at Home (Level I)

F

You needed some new shoes. You wanted a special kind. Your mother drove you to several different places before you found just the right shoes. Thank your mother for taking time to help you.

Assertiveness at Home (Level I)

G

You have a friend visiting. Your friend has been playing on your swing for a long time. Tell your friend that you want a turn now.

H

Your family has a nickname for you. It embarrasses you to be called that in front of other people. Tell your father that you don't want him to call you that nickname in front of others.

I

Go to a friend's house. Ask his/her mother if you can play with your friend.

J

You have been playing with a friend all afternoon. It is time for you to go home. Thank your friend's mother or father for letting you visit.

K

You have a friend visiting. He/she does not play carefully with your favorite toy. Ask your friend to be more careful.

Assertiveness at Home (Level I)

L

You bring a new friend to your house to play. Introduce your friend to your mother and father.

Assertiveness at Home (Level I)

M

You and your older brother get along well when you are alone together. But when his older friends come to your house, your brother teases you in front of them. Ask him not to tease you.

Assertiveness at Home (Level I)

N

ASSERTIVENESS AT HOME
(Level II)

Goal:

To practice courteous, assertive behavior in representative home situations.

Materials:

Cards (following; readability levels: A, 1.7; B, 2.2; C, 2.3; D, 2.3; E, 2.3; F, 2.2; G, 2.1; H, 2.5; *Spache Readability Formula*).

Procedure:

Elicit from the students the nonverbal and verbal signs of getting the message across confidently and courteously: standing tall, looking directly at a person, remembering courteous timing, using a courteous tone of voice, speaking clearly, using "I . . . ." Stress that assertiveness involves respecting oneself and respecting others.

Direct the students to form groups of two or three. Remind them to use the problem-solving process.

After each group role plays their solution, ask the class to critique the suggestion. Ask:

"How do you think that solution would work?"

"How would you have responded if _____ had said that to you?"

"Can you think of any other ways this might have been worked out satisfactorily?"

(Note: If a group of students model an aggressive or passive solution, ask them to try again, or ask someone else to model an assertive response before they try it again.)

For every role play, the test of assertiveness is: did the actor respect his/her own rights and the rights of others?

Your little brother has made something special for you. You know that he worked hard on it. Tell him how much you appreciate that.

Assertiveness at Home (Level II)

A

Your mother has planned a special dinner for your birthday. She tells you that she is going to fix a special cake for you. She doesn't know that you don't like that kind of cake. What will you do?

Assertiveness at Home (Level II)   B

Your older brother and sister frequently take your games out and play with them. They don't put them back. You feel angry about this, but you also know that you often borrow their things and don't return them. What will you do?

Assertiveness at Home (Level II)   C

You had a very disappointing day. Everything seemed to go wrong. Your parents are feeling sad for you, and they have been very thoughtful. They even did your chores for you. Tell them that you appreciate their thoughtfulness and caring.

Assertiveness at Home (Level II)   D

Your parents aren't home. You take some cookies that you were told not to take. You put them on a nice plate and then you stumble, dropping and breaking the plate. What will you say to your mother when she comes back?

Assertiveness at Home (Level II)   E

From *Games Children Should Play*,   © 1980, Mary K. Cihak and Barbara J. Heron, and Goodyear Publishing Co., Inc.

You are working on a special art project when your little brother comes in and takes some of your things. You chase after him. He falls and hurts himself. Just then your father comes in. What will you say?

Assertiveness at Home (Level II)   F

Your family and friends are eating Thanksgiving dinner at your aunt's house. You find that she has given you a dirty fork. What will you do?

Assertiveness at Home (Level II)   G

You are very uncomfortable around one of your relatives. You don't want to be left alone with him. Tell your parents how you feel, and ask them not to leave you alone with him.

Assertiveness at Home (Level II)   H

LANGUAGE ARTS / SOCIAL SCIENCE / HEALTH/SAFETY

ASSERTING YOUR RIGHT TO NOT GO ALONG WITH THE CROWD—PART I
(Level II)

Goal:

To recognize and practice one's right to assert oneself against group pressure.

202   Games Children Should Play

Materials:

Scripts (following); cards (following), one for each student (readability levels: A, 2.1; B, 2.5; C, 3.0; *Spache Readability Formula*).

Background:

Achieving group identity is a developmental stage, and it is not easy for young people to stand out as individuals. These exercises don't intend to eliminate the continual tension between group and individual goals,but they do intend to give children some basic practice in asserting their needs. For some young people, just forming the thought that they can act differently from peers is valuable growth.

Note that in each problem presented, the student is given the response to be role played. The object of this particular lesson is to practice saying "no," not to clarify values at this time.

Procedure:

Direct two students to practice the scripts before class time.

Develop readiness for this lesson by reviewing "What's Your Preference?" Chapter 5, using new topics such as roller skating or swimming; two current movies; two current actors; candy or fruit. Conclude by stating that individuals have the right to make different choices. Discuss with the class the importance of taking a stand against group pressure. Tell them that they have a right to stand up for what they believe or want, even when the rest of the group wants them to do something else. It is often difficult to say no to friends, but sometimes it can be really important to do so. This lesson will offer practice in ways to say "no" to friends when one needs to. Clarify that because a person chooses not to do what a friend wants does not mean that he/she has lost that friendship.

Direct the class to listen to each of the following scripts and predict the response that can be expected in each situation. Ask: What does each person feel? What does each want? What might happen next? Why?

After the scripts have been read and discussed, direct the students to form triads. Designate members A, B, C; then give each member of the triad the corresponding card. The groups will have three minutes for each situation. (Be sure to remind the students of their space limitations, and caution them that in the car situation, Card C, they are to demonstrate the words said in the situation, not the driving of the car.) Announce the end of each three-minute segment. When the triads have finished their practices, call the students back together in the larger group. Talk about each situation and ask for groups to volunteer to demonstrate the solutions that they thought were particularly effective. When discussing Card C, implant the idea that if all else fails, the student or gas attendant or operator could call upon the Highway Patrol for help.

ASSERTING YOUR RIGHT TO NOT GO
ALONG WITH THE CROWD
DEMONSTRATION SCRIPTS

1

Betty:
Hi, Lisa, do you want to go to the movie with me tonight? I've heard that it is a really good one.

Lisa:
Thanks a lot for asking me, Betty, but I don't want to go to that movie tonight. I surely appreciate your thinking of me, though.

Betty:
Oh, come on.

Lisa:
No, thanks anyway.

Betty:
Why not?

Lisa:
I'm really tired, and I just don't feel like going out tonight. But I'd like to go with you some other time.

Betty:
O.K., another time.

2

Lee:
Singh, I got some cigarettes. Let's go out back and smoke.

Singh:
I'm sorry, Lee, but I don't want to smoke.

Lee:
Oh, come on. It's not going to hurt you. What's the matter, are you afraid?

Singh:
No, Lee, I don't want to smoke. I appreciate your thinking of me, and I still want to be your friend, but I don't want to smoke.

Lee:
Gee whiz! Come on, it's no fun to smoke alone.

Singh:
I suppose it isn't, but I'm not going to smoke with you.

Lee:
I guess you aren't really my friend.

Singh:
Oh yes I am, I just won't smoke. I'd still like to see you at school and go to the movies on Saturday with you.

Games Children Should Play

Your friends want you to smoke with them. You don't want to. Tell them that you don't want to.

Asserting Your Right To Not Go Along With The Crowd (Level II)

A

Your friends want you to drink beer with them. You don't want to do that. Tell them that you don't want to do that, but you still want to be their friend.

Asserting Your Right To Not Go Along With The Crowd (Level II)

B

You're in a car with a driver who is driving very dangerously. You are scared. Tell the driver to stop at a gas station because you need to go to the bathroom. After you have gotten out of the car, tell the driver that you're not going to ride with him/her any longer. You'll find another way home. Then ask the gas attendant to let you use the phone. Call your parents, or if they're not home, a friend, and tell them the problem. Ask them to come get you.

Asserting Your Right to Not Go Along with the Crowd (Level II)

C

LANGUAGE ARTS / SOCIAL SCIENCE / HEALTH/SAFETY

ASSERTING YOUR RIGHT TO NOT GO ALONG WITH THE CROWD—PART II
(Level II)

Goal:

To recognize and practice one's right to assert oneself against group pressure.

From *Games Children Should Play,* © 1980, Mary K. Cihak and Barbara J. Heron, and Goodyear Publishing Co., Inc.

Materials:

Cards (following), one for each pair (readability levels: A, 2.2; B, 2.6; C, 2.5; D, 2.6; E, 2.9; (*Spache Readability Formula*).

Procedure:

Review the previous lesson, reminding students that they have a right to stand up for what they believe or want and that even though it is often difficult to say "no" to friends, it can be extremely important to do so. This lesson will offer further practice in ways to say "no" when one needs to. Remind students that because a person chooses not to do what a friend wants does not mean that he/she has lost that friendship.

Direct the students to form pairs. Give each pair a card. They will have three minutes to practice their situation. At the end of the practice period, call the students back together in a larger group. Talk about each situation and ask for pairs to volunteer to demonstrate solutions.

Your friend tells you that he/she can get drugs from an older brother. You are not interested. Tell your friend that you are not interested.

Asserting Your Right To Not Go Along With The Crowd—Part II (Level II)   **A**

Your friend wants you to hold your test paper so that he/she can copy your test answers. You don't want to do that. Tell your friend that he/she can't copy your paper.

Asserting Your Right To Not Go Along With The Crowd—Part II (Level II)   **B**

Your best friend wants to copy your homework. You do not want your friend to copy. Tell your friend that he/she will have to do his/her own work.

Asserting Your Right To Not Go Along With The Crowd—Part II (Level II)

C

Your friend wants to compare report cards. You don't want to share yours. Tell him/her that you are not going to tell your grades.

Asserting Your Right To Not Go Along With The Crowd—Part II (Level II)

D

Your friend wants to borrow your expensive guitar. You know that your friend does not have enough money to replace the guitar if it breaks. How will you tell your friend that you do not want him/her to borrow your guitar?

Asserting Your Right To Not Go Along With The Crowd—Part II (Level II)

E

LANGUAGE ARTS / SOCIAL SCIENCE / CONSUMER EDUCATION

TRAINING FOR YOUNG CONSUMERS: PRODUCT SITUATIONS
(Level II)

Goals:

To recognize reasonable consumer rights regarding quality of product.
To practice asserting consumer rights.

Materials:

Several copies of each card (following; readability levels: A, 2.7; B, 2.4; C, 2.8; D, 3.2; E, 2.0; F, 2.0; *Spache Readability Formula*).

Procedure:

Review the Problem-solving Process (p. 138). Discuss with students what a consumer can reasonably expect from a product that has been purchased. Talk about quality, workmanship, and comparative prices. Ask, for example: "Would it be reasonable to return a toy that you paid twenty-three cents for if it fell apart in three weeks?" "What if you paid thirteen dollars for a toy that fell apart in three weeks?"

Ask students to imagine that a product is not satisfactory and that they need to return it. What are some guides to remember in solving this problem? (Elicit: timing, courtesy, respect for others and for oneself and especially stating one's wants.)

Direct the students to form pairs. Give each pair a card. Ask them to role play for the class a respectful, assertive solution. As several role plays are demonstrated, draw students' attention to the fact that there isn't just one good way to solve a problem.

Again, the test of assertiveness is: did the solution show respect for one's own rights and the rights of others?

You purchased a pair of shoes, and within two weeks the soles separated from the tops. Show how you would return them and ask for a replacement.

Training for Young Consumers: Product Situations (Level II)

A

You purchased a toy. It fell apart within two days. The clerk wants to give you a different one, but you've decided that you want to have your money back. Tell the clerk that.

Training for Young Consumers: Product Situations (Level II)

B

You are in a restaurant with some friends, and you order a hamburger. When you bite into it, you realize it isn't cooked on the inside. Explain the problem to the waitress/waiter, and ask to have it cooked well-done.

Training for Young Consumers: Product Situations (Level II)

C

You purchased a kite from a store. You expected it to be like all the other kites you have and to fall apart within two days. But this kite lasts two weeks, and you are really pleased. Go back to the store where you bought it and ask for the manager. Tell the manager what you think of this kite, and thank her/him for stocking this brand.

Training for Young Consumers: Product Situations (Level II)

D

You purchased a model airplane kit. On the cover it said, "Easy to assemble. Simple directions." When you opened the box, there were twenty pages of directions you couldn't understand. Return the kit to the store and explain the problem. Tell them what you want.

Training for Young Consumers: Product Situations (Level II)

E

In your favorite magazine, you saw an advertisement for a skateboard. You sent for it. It fell apart in two weeks. Write a letter to the company requesting your money back. Write a letter to the magazine, telling them your experience.

Training for Young Consumers: Product Situations (Level II)

F

TRAINING FOR YOUNG CONSUMERS: SERVICE SITUATIONS
(Level II)

Goals:

To recognize reasonable consumer rights with regard to service. To practice asserting consumer rights.

Materials:

Several copies of each of the cards (following; readability levels: A, 2.8; B, 2.6; C, 2.0; D, 3.1; E, 2.5; F, 2.8; *Spache Readability Formula*).

Procedure:

Review the lessons on "Guess What Happens"(p. 145). Recall that "victims" can often change others' behaviors by changing their own behavior. Remind students that people usually repeat actions when they receive a response that they like.

Explain: In consumer relationships, poor service continues because consumers ignore it. Good service is often neglected.

Ask the students to form pairs. Give each pair a card. Direct them to role play for the class an assertive, courteous solution.

During the discussion of the role plays include consideration of the feelings and problems that clerks and waiters/waitresses have.

You go to the store to buy something special, and you have a hard time finding the right thing. The clerk has been very helpful and courteous to you. Call (or ask to speak to) the manager of the store. Tell the manager about your experience with the clerk and how much you appreciated the clerk's help. Tell the manager that you think that he/she has a good employee.

Training for Young Consumers: Service Situations (Level II)   A

You are in a store. The clerk waits on everyone who comes in after you (they are adults), and only waits on you after all the adults have left the store. Tell the clerk how you feel.

Training for Young Consumers: Service Situations (Level II)

B

You are in a store. The clerk waits on everyone who comes in (they are adults), and waits on you only after all the adults have left the store. This has happened before, and you spoke to the clerk about it last week. Speak to the manager and tell him/her your complaint.

Training for Young Consumers: Service Situations (Level II)

C

You have taken your bicycle in to the shop to be repaired. Later when you take it home, you find that the problem still exists. You take the bike back to the shop. The clerk is rude and says that it was fixed and that you must have done something to ruin it. Remain courteous, but continue to firmly insist on having it repaired correctly.

Training for Young Consumers: Service Situations (Level II)

D

You have been wanting a certain game for several weeks. You go to the store and find that it is less expensive than you expected. Tell the clerk how pleased you are with the price.

Training for Young Consumers: Service Situations (Level II)

E

You have been waiting in line for a movie for about thirty minutes. People in front of you let several people cut into the line. Tell the people who cut in how you feel and what you want them to do.

Training for Young Consumers: Service Situations (Level II)

F

LANGUAGE ARTS / SOCIAL STUDIES

USING THE TELEPHONE
(Levels I and II)

Goals:

To become aware of the need to consider timing and courtesy when using the telephone. To practice good timing, courtesy, and assertiveness when using the telephone.

Materials:

Practice telephones lend a reality that is helpful but not essential to these lessons.

Procedure:

Review the need for courtesy and timing when communicating with people. Point out that it is harder to consider good timing when using the telephone because we can't see what the other people are doing. Because we can't see into their homes and because the telephone disturbs everyone at their home, we have to follow some general guidelines.

Attempt to elicit from the students general times when most people *don't* like to be disturbed: before breakfast—before 8:00 A.M.; on weekends—before 9:00 A.M.; at meal times—and between 5:30 P.M. and 7:00 P.M.; and after they have gone to bed—or after 9:00 P.M.

Summarize that in most cases, the best times to call are in the middle of the morning or in the afternoon (unless there are small children who might be napping) and in the early evening.

Teach children that courtesy on the telephone means:

1. Identifying yourself, whether you are the caller or the person receiving the call.

2. Using the courtesy words of "please" and "thank you," "hello," "good-bye."

Select a volunteer to help you to model the first telephone call for the students.

Student:
Hello, this is Jamie speaking.

Teacher:
Hello, Jamie, this is Mrs. Taylor calling.

Teacher:
May I speak with your mother, please?

Student:
Hello, Mrs. Taylor. Just a minute, I'll call my mother.

Teacher:
Thank you, Jamie.

Attempt to give every child a chance to "talk on the telephone." Direct two children at a time to talk—one child to go to the front of the room and the other to the back. Each child turns his/her back to the other so that they may not see each other but only hear each other. They can communicate only with words.

Use the following situations for practice in using good timing and courtesy words. After each demonstration, discuss whether good timing and courtesy were used. The children then practice the following phone calls:

Telephone your friend. When his/her mother answers, ask if this is a convenient time to talk with your friend.

Telephone your friend and ask if you may get a ride to school tomorrow because something is wrong with your parents' car.

Telephone your mother's work place. Ask to speak with her.

Answer the telephone. Tell the caller that your father isn't at home. Tell him that you expect your father about six o'clock, if he would like to call back.

Answer the telephone. Tell the caller that your sister isn't at home. Ask if you may give her a message.

Answer the telephone. Your father's friend is calling for him. Tell your father that he has a phone call.

Answer the telephone. Someone is calling for your mother. Tell the caller that your mother is eating dinner now. Ask if she can call him/her back.

From *Games Children Should Play*,   © 1980, Mary K. Cihak and Barbara J. Heron, and Goodyear Publishing Co., Inc.

TRAINING FOR REPORTING EMERGENCIES
(Levels I and II)

Goal:

To practice effectively reporting emergencies.

Materials:

Simulated telephones or play telephones if possible. Chart: Guide to Reporting Emergencies.

Procedure:

Talk about how to report an emergency. Tell the students that there are several things they must remember to do when reporting emergencies. Discuss the procedures listed on the following guide:

GUIDE TO REPORTING EMERGENCIES

1. Give your name and address.
2. Tell what the situation is and where it is happening.
3. STAY ON THE TELEPHONE UNTIL YOU ARE TOLD TO HANG UP.

If your area is using a general emergency phone number, teach that number. If you don't have that number, teach students that they can always dial "O" if they can't find the emergency number.

Teach children that if they are reporting a fire, they must first leave that building before calling the fire department.

Model the following emergency telephone call, either as a monologue or with a helper.

Miss Smith:

My house is on fire. This is Miss Smith. I am at 612 Main Street. The fire is at 617 Main Street. The phone I am calling from is 333-1146.

Operator:

All right, Miss Smith, I'll call the fire department. Please stay on the line.

Discuss how you followed the steps in "Guide to Reporting Emergencies."

Have each of the students practice one of the following situations. The reporting student sits behind the class with his/her back towards them, so that he/she must rely solely upon words. The teacher, acting as operator, sits across the room from the caller. After each practice, discuss whether the caller followed each of the three steps in "Guide" above.

SITUATIONS:

Call an ambulance because your grandmother has fallen and can't get up. She may have broken a leg.

Call the fire department to report a fire in the garage of the apartments across the street.

Call the fire department to report a fire. You don't know the address where you are. (Be prepared to give prominent landmarks or neighbors' names.)

There is a fire in your kitchen. Be sure everyone is out of your house, then call the fire department from the neighbor's house to report the fire.

You look out the window of your house and see three men jump on an old man and steal his money. Call the police.

Your father is trapped under the car and is hurt. Call an ambulance.

You are calling the fire department and receive a busy signal. Dial the operator and tell him/her your problem.

You are baby-sitting and discover that the three-year-old has gotten into the medicine cabinet and has taken several aspirin. The child is pale and cold. Call the doctor, then the parents.

You see that an accident has happened in the street in front of your house. Someone is lying in the street, bleeding and unconscious. Call an ambulance.

You look out your back window and see a man who doesn't live in your neighborhod crawling in the neighbor's window. Call the police.

Your father has seriously cut himself. Mother is driving him to the doctor. Call the doctor and tell him/her what happened and to expect them to arrive there within five minutes.

Follow-up:

Copy the Guide to Reporting Emergencies.

LANGUAGE / SOCIAL SCIENCE / HEALTH/SAFETY

RECOGNIZING POTENTIALLY DANGEROUS SITUATIONS
(Levels I and II)

Goals:

To recognize some common clues that might indicate a potentially dangerous situation. To understand ways in which to prevent danger.

From *Games Children Should Play,*   © 1980, Mary K. Cihak and Barbara J. Heron, and Goodyear Publishing Co., Inc.

Materials:

Scripts (following).

Background:

This lesson is included in order to teach students to be alert to the warning signs of potentially dangerous situations. The teacher's attitude is crucial here: if the teacher overdramatizes the situations or acts fearful, fear and anxiety are what is taught rather than confidence and the ability to deal appropriately with situations.

In teaching this lesson, emphasize that learning to be alert to *possible* warnings and learning how to handle potentially dangerous situations helps people to be more confident.

Procedure:

Tell the students that often people find themselves in dangerous situations because they didn't recognize some early warning signs. People can protect themselves more effectively if they are alerted by early warnings of possible problems. Explain that by the end of this lesson they should be able to tell the difference between the *need to be alert* and the *need to act*.

Tell the students that you are going to read some scripts to them. They are to imagine that they are the student in each situation.

When they hear the first clue that they need to be alert because there *might* be a problem in the situation, they are to raise one thumb.

When they hear a second clue that the situation has the potential for being dangerous, they are to raise two thumbs.

When they are sure that the situation has become dangerous enough that they must do something about it, they are to put their hands in their laps.

Indicate that some of the situations you read will not be serious. Students will need to listen to recognize the difference between ordinary and potentially dangerous situations, that is, the difference between being merely alert, and needing to act. As each monologue is read, discuss what the warning clues were (if any), then discuss choices for appropriate action. Clarify that in a dangerous situation the first and highest priority is *safety*. Respect for the other person becomes unimportant. Conclude the discussion by summarizing that clues to potentially dangerous situations include:

The asking of personal questions (name, address, destination).

The suggestion that the student go someplace with the person.

Reasonable solutions to such situations include:

Avoiding giving personal information.

Moving away.

Telling an adult.

Calling out for help.

Being sure to tell parents about the situation.

Remind students that they can be confident and comfortable with people, particularly when they know how to deal with many different situations.

RECOGNIZING POTENTIALLY DANGEROUS SITUATIONS
SCRIPTS

NOTE TO TEACHER:
The number (1) after a sentence indicates the first clue that the situation might become dangerous. Students should hold up one thumb. The number (2) after a sentence indicates a second warning that the situation might become dangerous. Students should hold up two thumbs. The number (3) after a sentence indicates that the situation has become dangerous enough that they must do something about it. Students indicate this by putting their hands in their laps. Notice that sometimes there are not two warnings. Some of the situations will not be dangerous, and therefore no action would be needed by the student.

1

SITUATION:
You are in the park flying your kite, and a stranger approaches. He/she says:

> "Hi! Isn't this a nice day?
>
> Are you out here in the park all by yourself? (1)
>
> Do you like chocolate candy? (2)
>
> Why don't you come with me? (3)
>
> I have some in the car."

REASONABLE SOLUTION:
Don't go. Quickly move far enough away that you can't be reached, and say "No, thank you."

2

SITUATION:
You are sitting alone in the back of a half-empty bus, and a stranger comes near. He/she says:

> "I see you're sitting back here in the bus by yourself.
>
> Mind if I sit with you? (1)
>
> Where are you going? (2)
>
> Look at that 'neat' car out there." (Puts hand on knee of student.) (3)

REASONABLE SOLUTION:
Immediately get up and move away to the front of the bus, near the driver.

3

SITUATION:
You are playing in the park. An adult walks up and says:

> "Say, that's a real nice soccer ball. (1)
>
> You're really lucky to have a leather one like that.
>
> It's a good day for playing soccer, isn't it?
>
> So long."

REASONABLE SOLUTION:
This appears not to be a dangerous situation; therefore, no action is needed.

4

SITUATION:
The movie that you attended finished after dark in the evening. (1) You are walking on the sidewalk. A person comes up to you and says:

> "It's a pretty dark night, isn't it?
>
> What's your name? (2)
>
> Do you like dogs? I do, too.
>
> I have the cutest new pup. He's round and furry and lots of fun to play with. Do you have any pets?
>
> Do you want to come see my dog?" (3)

REASONABLE SOLUTION:
Don't give your name. Say, "No, thanks," and move on quickly.

5

SITUATION:
You are waiting after school for your mom to pick you up. A car pulls up and the driver says:

> "Hi there. How are you? (1)
>
> I'm a friend of your mom's.
>
> She told me to pick you up. (2)
>
> I'll take you home. Hop in." (3)

REASONABLE SOLUTION:
Don't go until you've called your mother to find out if it is true that you are to go home with that person. Go to the school office to use the phone. Explain the circumstances to an adult there.

SITUATION:
You are riding your bike. An adult who is also biking pulls up beside you and says:

"Hi! Say, I just noticed your bike. It looks as though you are getting a flat tire.

I have a pump here.

Would you like me to pump it up a bit for you? (1)

There you go—that will hold it until you get to a station for more air.

You'd better do that soon, though.

So long."

REASONABLE SOLUTION:
This appears not to be a dangerous situation; therefore, no action is needed.

SITUATION:
You and your mom are home. Someone knocks on the door. You don't recognize the person, and you don't open the door.

"I'm from the gas company.

I need to come inside to talk with you about your bill." (3)

REASONABLE SOLUTION:
Ask him/her to slip his/her identification under the door, and call the gas company to make sure that the person was supposed to come to see you.

SITUATION:
You meet a friend of your parents downtown. He/she says:

"Hi there. How have you been?

How are your folks?

Say, why don't you come with me to my house and go swimming with me? (1)

No one else is home." (3)

REASONABLE SOLUTION:
Tell him/her that you'll check with your parents and see if they can come with you. Don't go without first checking with your parents.

SITUATION:
You answer the telephone and a voice says:

"Hi, is your mom home?

Where has she gone? (1)

Are you kids home alone?" (3)

REASONABLE SOLUTION:
Don't answer personal questions. Hang up unless you know and trust the person.

LANGUAGE ARTS / SAFETY

USING THE TELEPHONE IN POTENTIALLY DANGEROUS SITUATIONS
(Levels I and II)

Goal:

To practice assertive skills in difficult telephone situations.

Materials:

Scripts (following). It is helpful, but not essential, to have practice telephones for this lesson.

Procedure:

Prior to this lesson, with a volunteer, practice the script.

Discuss with the students that there are times when even though one needs to be courteous, one shouldn't give a caller all the information he/she wants. Discuss the importance of not revealing to strangers that you are at home alone. Explain that in some situations, protection is more important than courtesy. If callers refuse to identify themselves, it is safest to hang up.

In these situations, it is important that the teacher or another adult player plays the caller, so that the students can practice being assertive with adults.

Read the scripts with the volunteer. After each script, discuss the role of the student. Did the student recognize a potentially dangerous situation? Did he/she handle the situation without revealing more than he/she should have? Was the student as courteous as possible?

When the scripts have been modeled, read each of the following situations. Choose volunteers to practice them. Discuss each role play in terms of safety, assertiveness, and courtesy. Give as many students as possible a chance to practice. Be sure that students understand that they should report to their parents all unusual phone calls.

You are alone. You have been told not to tell anyone that you're alone. Someone calls. Tell that person that your mother can't come to the phone now. Ask if you may take a number and have her call back.

The operator calls and says he/she has a collect phone call and asks if you will accept the charges. Tell the operator that you'll have to get your mother (or father), and ask him/her to wait a minute.

You answer the phone, and all you hear at the other end are squeaky noises. Say hello again, but then if the noises continue, hang up the phone.

You answer the phone and a scary voice says, "Hello, Cutie, are you home alone?" Hang up the phone immediately. (Tell your parents what happened, or phone a neighbor and tell what happened.)

From *Games Children Should Play*, © 1980, Mary K. Cihak and Barbara J. Heron, and Goodyear Publishing Co., Inc.

USING THE TELEPHONE IN POTENTIALLY
DANGEROUS SITUATIONS
SCRIPTS

1

SCENE:
Kim is alone. Her mother has gone shopping and expects to be back in
a half hour.

(telephone rings)

Kim:
Hello, this is Kim speaking.

Caller:
Hello, Kim, is your mother home?

Kim:
Who is calling, please?

Caller:
I said, is your mother home?

Kim:
I'm sorry, I don't recognize your voice. Who are you?

Caller:
(angrily) Kim, I want to talk to your mother.
Kim hangs up.

2

SCENE:
Carlos is home alone.

(telephone rings)

Carlos:
Hello, this is Carlos.

Caller:
Hello, Carlos, how are you?

Carlos:
Fine, thank you. Who's calling, please?

Caller:
This is Mr. Felix. You don't know me, but I know your dad. Is your dad
home?

Carlos:
I'm sorry, Mr. Felix, he can't come to the phone right now. Could I take
a message?

Mr. Felix:
Where does your dad work, Carlos?

Carlos:
In town.

Mr. Felix:
What does he do?

Carlos:
He works.

Mr. Felix:
(Laughs a little.) Does he make a lot of money?

Carlos:
Could I take a message for you, Mr. Felix?

Mr. Felix:
What time does he go to work?

Carlos:
I'm sorry, Mr. Felix, I have to go now. Goodbye. (Hangs up.)

LANGUAGE ARTS / SOCIAL STUDIES / CONSUMER EDUCATION / ART

A CELEBRATION: ADVERTISING OURSELVES!
(Levels I and II)

Goal:

To increase positive references to oneself.

Materials:

Magazines; newspapers; poster-size paper; crayons; scissors; paste.

Procedure:

Briefly discuss the purpose of advertising, showing common examples from magazines and newspapers. Elicit from students the fact that advertisements use positive words and colorful pictures to get their messages across.

Tell the students that you believe each one of them has personal characteristics and talents worth advertising. Give examples.

Direct the students to think for a moment about their attributes. Then distribute newspapers and magazines with the instruction that each person is to create a poster advertising himself/herself. They may use words and pictures cut from the magazines and newspapers to create a collage describing their "best self."

Post the advertisements on classroom bulletin boards.

Variations:

On a large mural-sized paper, the entire class creates an "Advertisement for Our Class," advertising the talents and characteristics of the group.

The most effective single word in advertising is "You." ("You asked for it . . . you got it"; "You, you're the one . . . .") Students may do a take-off on the "you asked for it" theme: "You got me . . . ; I'm, I'm the one . . ." (with the largest freckles, with the most books read, etc.).

FEEDBACK FORM FOR CHAPTER 7

This week I remembered to use good timing when I _____

_____

_____.

This week I was courteous when I _____

_____

_____.

I am going to use courteous words when _____

_____

_____.

_____

(Name)

FEEDBACK FORM FOR CHAPTER 7

When I am angry, I need to remember to _____

_____.

It is hard for me to _____

_____.

I am going to try to _____

_____.

_____

(Name)

Celebrating the Year's End

Activities in this chapter conclude the school year or mark the end of this communications training in the classroom. They are in fact a celebration of the students' growth as individuals and as an increasingly cohesive or supportive group.

In both Levels I and II, the "Who Am I?" papers are removed from their hidden storage place after the students have completed a current version. The teacher guides a group discussion centering upon the difference between the two versions. In a similar exercise, the teacher provides time for students to reread their journals.

Besides these exercises, Level II students make a group collage that highlights the ways in which they have grown together as a class.

This chapter's feedback form includes a form on which you, the teacher, may wish to give positive feedback to each student.

LANGUAGE ARTS

CONCLUSION TO THE JOURNAL
(Levels I and II)

Goal:

To review the year by reading one's own journal.

Procedure:

Allow fifteen to twenty minutes for students to silently read their journals.

(Level II)

For Level II, at the end of the reading period, write on the blackboard the following open-ended sentences, which comprise the last journal entry for the year:

227

During the year, these things were fun: _____
_____.
During the year, I didn't like _____
_____.
During the year, I learned _____
_____.
During the year, I decided _____
_____.
During the year, these people were my friends: _____
_____.
When I read through my journal, I feel

I feel _____because _____.
I feel _____because _____.

(Level I)

For Level I, at the end of the review/reading period, lead students in responding in turn to the following open-ended sentences:

This year, I had fun doing _____.
This year, I learned _____.
This year, I made friends with _____.

LANGUAGE ARTS

WHO AM I—NOW?
(Levels I and II)

Goal:

To recognize one's growth since the beginning of the school year.

Materials:

One copy of "Who Am I?" Level I (p. 12) or Level II (p. 16) duplicated for each student.

228

Procedure:

Distribute the blank copies of the "Who Am I?" worksheet. Direct students to complete the blanks according to how they feel and think about things today.

Distribute the original "Who Am I?" papers that have been stored all year. Allow students time in which to compare the original paper with today's thoughts.

Volunteers may wish to share ways in which they have changed and grown through the year.

Follow-up:

Direct students to write in their journals:

I used to _____

and now I _____.

LANGUAGE ARTS / SOCIAL STUDIES / ART

A CELEBRATION FOR THE YEAR'S END: WHERE WE'VE BEEN
(Level II)

Goal:

To celebrate the ways in which students have grown through the year.

Materials:

Magazines; newspapers; large poster paper (mural-size); crayons; scissors; paste; soft background music.

Procedure:

Discuss the idea of growth, stressing the growth individuals have made through the school year. Include growth in everything from mathematical knowledge to increased height to new friendships to sports prowess. Refer to the newly reopened "Who Am I?" pages for a guide to discussion.

Focus the discussion on evaluating the growth of the class throughout this course. Consider ways students listen and speak to each other; how teacher and students work together; how each one feels about himself/herself; how the class has solved problems together.

Discuss, too, the hopes the students have for the following years: What do they hope to learn? How do they wish to improve their lives?

Divide the empty mural into three large sections, labeling them:

WHERE WE'VE BEEN (our class at the beginning of the year)	*WHERE WE ARE* (what we've learned)	*WHERE WE'RE GOING* (hopes for later years)

As soft music plays, students remain in silence at their desks or seated on the floor with magazines. When they find a contribution to make to one section, they add it to the mural, returning to their places.

If desired, a class party follows.

FEEDBACK FORM FOR CHAPTER 8

Dear Teacher,

My favorite memory of this school year is _____

_____.

I liked _____

_____.

I learned _____

_____.

Thank you for _____

_____.

Sincerely,

_____
(Name)

From *Games Children Should Play,*   © 1980, Mary K. Cihak and Barbara J. Heron, and Goodyear Publishing Co., Inc.

FEEDBACK FORM
FROM TEACHER TO STUDENT

Dear _____,

    My favorite memory of you this school year is _____

_____.

    I liked _____

_____.

    Thank you for _____

_____.

                          Sincerely,

                          _____
                                 (teacher)

From *Games Children Should Play*, © 1980, Mary K. Cihak and Barbara J. Heron, and Goodyear Publishing Co., Inc.

Bibliography

ALBERTI, ROBERT and MICHAEL L. EMMONS. *Your Perfect Right: A Guide to Assertive Behavior*. San Luis Obispo, Ca.: Impact, 1974.

BACH, GEORGE ROBERT and YETTA M. BERNHARD. *Aggression Lab: The Fair Fight Training Manual*. Dubuque, Iowa: Kendall-Hunt, 1971.

BACH, GEORGE and HERB GOLDBERG. *Creative Aggression*. Garden City, N.Y.: Doubleday, 1974.

BACH, GEORGE and PETER WYDEN. *The Intimate Enemy: How to Fight Fair in Love and Marriage*. N.Y.: Morrow, 1969.

BROWN, GEORGE ISAAC. *Human Teaching for Human Learning*. N.Y.: Viking, 1971.

CHASE, LARRY. *The Other Side of the Report Card*. Santa Monica, Ca.: Goodyear, 1975.

CHESLER, MARK and ROBERT FOX. *Role-Playing Methods in the Classroom*. Chicago: Science Research Associates, 1966.

CLEAVER, ELDRIDGE. *Soul On Ice*. N.Y.: Dell, 1968.

DREIKURS, RUDOLF. *Psychology in the Classroom*. N.Y.: Harper & Row, 1957.

FENSTERHEIM, HERBERT. *Don't Say Yes When You Want to Say No: How Assertiveness Training Can Change Your Life*. N.Y.: McKay, 1975.

FREED, ALVYN. *T.A. For Tots*. Sacramento: Jalmar, 1973.

FREED, ALVYN. *T.A. For Kids*. Sacramento: Jalmar, 1971.

GAZDA, GEORGE M. et al. *Human Relations Development*. Boston: Allyn and Bacon, 1977.

GLASSER, WILLIAM. *Reality Therapy*. N.Y.: Harper & Row, 1965.

GLASSER, WILLIAM. *Schools Without Failure*. N.Y.: Harper & Row, 1969.

GORDON, THOMAS. *Parent Effectiveness Training*. N.Y.: Wyden, 1970.

GORDON, THOMAS (with Noel Burch). *T.E.T., Teacher Effectiveness Training*. N.Y.: Wyden, 1974.

HAWLEY, ROBERT, SIDNEY P. SIMON, and DAVID D. BRITTON. *Composition for Personal Growth: Values Clarification through Writing*. N.Y.: Hart, 1973.

HAWLEY, ROBERT C. and ISABEL HAWLEY. *Human Values in the Classroom: A Handbook for Teachers*. N.Y.: Hart, 1975.

HAWLEY, ROBERT C. *Value Exploration through Role Playing: Practical Strategies for Use in the Classroom*. N.Y.: Hart, 1975.

HUNTER, MADELINE C. *Motivation Theory for Teachers: A Programmed Book*. El Segundo, Ca.: TIP Publications, 1967.

HUNTER, MADELINE C. *Reinforcement Theory for Teachers: A Programmed Book*. El Segundo, Ca.: TIP Publications, 1967.

HUNTER, MADELINE C. *Retention Theory for Teachers: A Programmed Book*. El Segundo, Ca.: TIP Publications, 1967.

HUNTER, MADELINE C. *Teach More—Faster! A Programmed Book*. El Segundo, Ca.: TIP Publications, 1967.

HUNTER, MADELINE C. *Teach for Transfer: A Programmed Book*. El Segundo, Ca.: TIP Publications, 1971.

HUNTER, MADELINE C. and DOUG RUSSELL. "Planning for Effective Instruction" (Lesson Design), 1976.

JOSLIN, SESYLE, *What Do You Say, Dear?* N.Y.: Young Scott Books, 1958.

KOHLBERG, LAWRENCE and ELLIOTT TURIEL, eds. *Recent Research in Moral Development*. N.Y.: Holt, Rinehart and Winston, 1971.

LEONARD, GEORGE B. *Education and Ecstasy*. N.Y.: Dell, 1968.

MERRILL, HARMIN. *People Project*. Menlo Park, Ca.: Wesley, 1973.

PIAGET, JEAN. *The Moral Judgment of the Child*. N.Y.: The Free Press, 1965.

POSTMAN, NEIL and CHARLES WEINGARTNER. *Teaching as a Subversive Activity*. N.Y.: Delacorte, 1969.

SEATTLE PUBLIC SCHOOL DISTRICT #1. *Rainbow Activities, 50 Multicultural/Human Relations Experiences*. South El Monte, Ca.: Creative Teaching Press, 1977.

SHAFTEL, FANNIE R. and GEORGE SHAFTEL. *Role-Playing for Social Values: Decision-Making in the Social Studies*. Englewood Cliffs, N.J.: Prentice-Hall, 1967.

SIMON, SIDNEY B., LELAND W. HOWE, and HOWARD KIRSCHENBAUN. *Values Clarification: A Handbook of Practical Strategies for Teachers and Students*. N.Y.: Hart, 1972.

SMITH, MANUEL J. *When I Say No, I Feel Guilty—Using the Skills of Systematic Assertive Therapy*. N.Y.: Dial, 1979.

SPOLIN, VIOLA. *Improvisation in the Theatre*. Evanston, Ill.: Northwestern University Press, 1963.

ROBERT, MARC. *Loneliness in the Schools*. Nills, Ill.: Argus Communications, 1973.

THOMPSON, JAMES J. *Beyond Words: Nonverbal Communication in the Classroom*. N.Y.: Citation Press, 1973.

Appendix

FEELINGS THAT CHILDREN HAVE BUT CANNOT ALWAYS IDENTIFY

Angry
Annoyed
Anxious
Astounded

Bored
Brave

Calm
Cheated
Confused
Cruel

Different
Disturbed

Energetic
Excited
Exhausted

Fascinated
Fearful
Frantic
Foolish
Frustrated
Frightened
Free

Glad
Good
Guilty

Happy
Helpful
Helpless
Homesick
Horrible
Hurt

Ignored

Jealous
Joyous

Kind

Lazy
Left out
Lonely
Low

Mad
Mean
Miserable

Naughty
Nervous
Nice

Overwhelmed

Panicked
Peaceful

Petrified
Picked on
Pleased
Pretty
Proud

Refreshed
Rejected
Relaxed
Relieved
Restless

Sad
Scared
Shocked
Silly
Sneaky
Startled
Stupid

Tense
Terrible
Tired

Upset

Violent

Worried

From *Games Children Should Play*, © 1980, Mary K. Cihak and Barbara J. Heron, and Goodyear Publishing Co., Inc.

ADDITIONAL TOPICS FOR JOURNAL WRITING

Self-Awareness:

I'm feeling _____ because _____ .

I'm feeling _____ because I _____ .

I'm feeling _____ because I _____ and I'd like to _____ .

I feel angry when _____ .

I would be happier if I _____ .

I used to be _____ . Now I _____ .

I wish I _____ .

If I were a man, I _____ .

If I were a woman, I _____ .

The last time I felt powerful, I felt _____ .

I don't understand _____ .

One problem I have is _____ .

I'm glad I _____ .

I'm sorry I _____ .

I get angry when I _____ .

I had these opposite feelings, _____ and _____ , when I _____ .

I find it hard to imagine myself _____ .

I wish I could tell _____ that I _____ .

I wonder _____ .

I worry _____ .

Listening:

I am going to show _____ that I am really listening to him/her.

When people don't listen to me, I feel _____ .

When _____ listens to me I feel _____ .

I wish _____ would listen to me because _____ .

I plan to listen better to _____ , so that he/she will feel _____ .

When I don't listen to _____ , he/she probably feels _____ .

Self-Image:

Some things that I like about myself are _____ .

I am proud of myself because I _____ .

I can _____ .

236   Games Children Should Play

I wish I could _____ .

If I could be anything I wanted to be, I would be _____ .

If I could do anything I wanted to do, I would _____ .

Nonverbal:

Sometimes I show people how I feel by _____ .

When I'm feeling _____ , I show it by _____ .

Following Class Discussion:

During the class meeting I felt _____ because I _____ .

During the class activity I noticed _____ .

When I am in a group discussion, I feel _____ . I speak _____ .

If I could change one thing about this class, it would be _____ .

The best part of this class period was _____ .

I find it hard to give my ideas when _____ .

I find it easy to give my ideas when _____ .

When we did the activity today, I learned _____ .

When we were working together today, I felt _____ .

Some ideas that I have on _____ are _____ .

Goal setting:

One thing I'm going to do to make this class better is to _____ .

By next month I hope to learn to _____ .

In ten years I hope I _____ .

I want to learn _____ .

When I grow up, I'd like to be _____ .

One thing about myself I'd really like to change is _____ .

    I'll start changing by _____ .

By (name of month) I want to be able to _____ .

    I will know I have done it by _____ .

    I'll celebrate it by _____ .

I'm going to show respect to _____ by _____ .

Today I made progress in _____ by _____ .

I did my best work today in _____ .

Tomorrow I want to improve my work in _____ by _____ .

From *Games Children Should Play*, © 1980, Mary K. Cihak and Barbara J. Heron, and Goodyear Publishing Co., Inc.

When I read my journal, I learned that I _____ .

When I read my journal, I remembered _____ .

I feel _____ when I read my journal today because _____ .

ART

A CELEBRATION: THE CHRISTMAS ORNAMENT
(Levels I and II)

Goals:

To increase self-image. To make something for parents.

Materials:

Photograph of each child; construction paper; crayons; scissors; pens; paste; yarn; laminating machine.

Procedure:

Direct each student to:

1. Cut the face out of his/her photograph.
2. On scratch paper, design an ornament around the face (Santa Claus, reindeer, rabbit, elf, jack-in-the-box, angel, etc.).
3. Copy the design on construction paper. Paste the face on the design, and color in the rest of the design.
4. Write his/her name and the date on the back of the ornament.
5. Make a hole for a yarn hanger.
6. Laminate the ornament.
7. Tie a piece of colored yarn through the hole.

The ornament is ready for hanging on a Christmas tree.

ADDITIONAL FEEDBACK FORMS

After this lesson I felt:

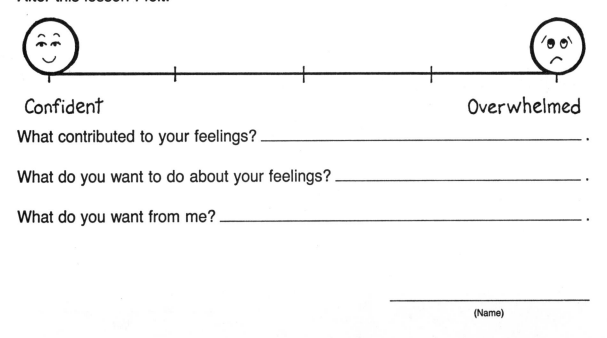

Happy   Unhappy

What contributed to your feelings? _____.

What do you want to do about your feelings? _____.

What do you want from me? _____.

_____
(Name)

After this lesson I felt:

Confident   Overwhelmed

What contributed to your feelings? _____.

What do you want to do about your feelings? _____.

What do you want from me? _____.

_____
(Name)

Appendix   **239**

From *Games Children Should Play*,   © 1980, Mary K. Cihak and Barbara J. Heron, and Goodyear Publishing Co., Inc.

After this lesson I felt:

Knowledgeable   Confused

What contributed to your feelings? _____.

What do you want to do about your feelings? _____.

What do you want from me? _____.

_____
(Name)

How comfortable are you doing the following activities?

	0*	1**	2	3	4	5***

Writing in your journal   _____

Sharing your ideas in a class
  meeting   _____

Listening to other people's ideas   _____

*What's that?

**I'd rather have homework.

***I like it and I can do it.

_____
(Name)